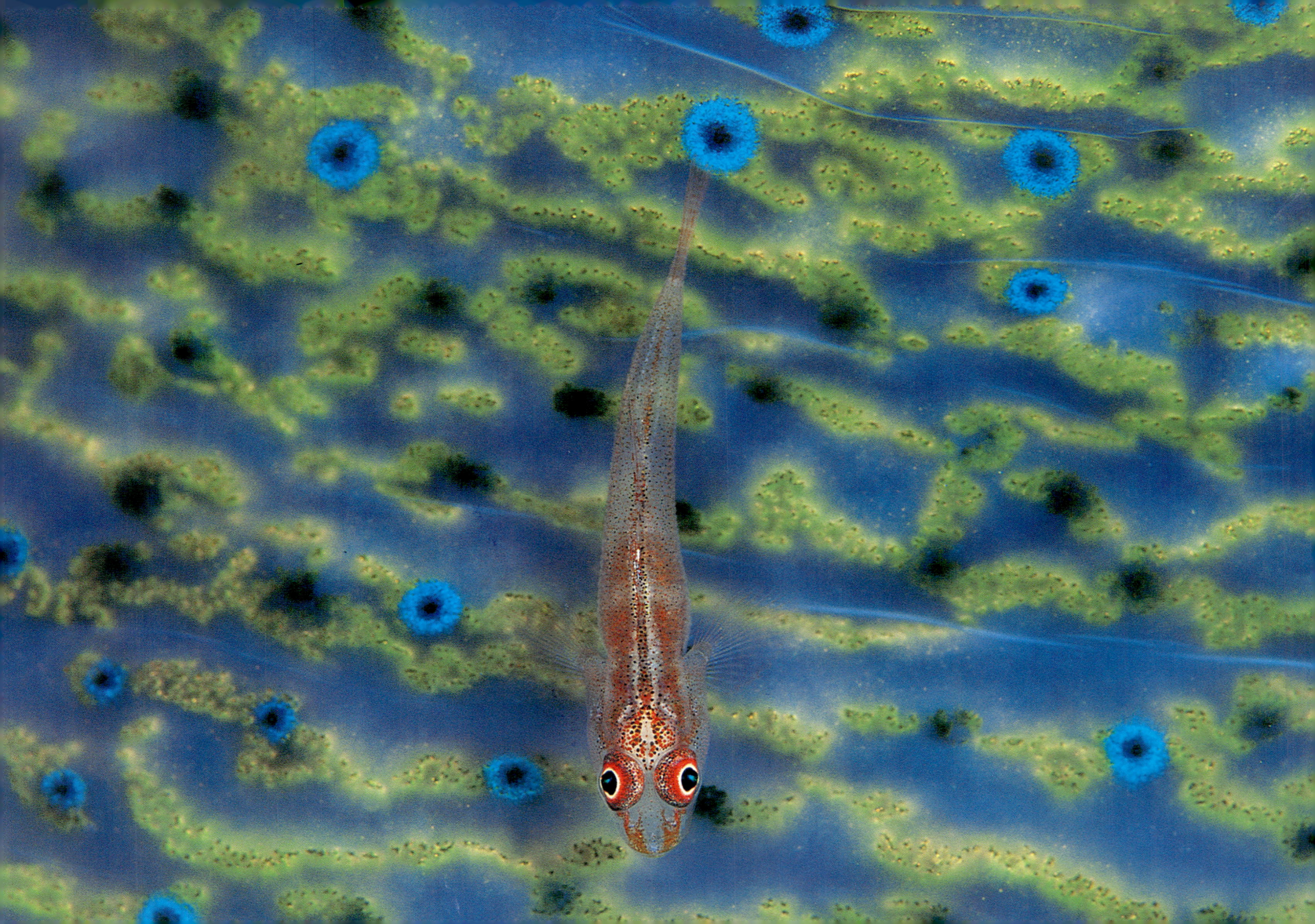

# australia's
## natural treasures

with recipes from paradise

chantal dunbar

*For Dominique and Daryl*
*Thank you for your unwavering support, unconditional love and*
*most of all – for believing in me when I lost faith.*

Published by: Laughing Waters, PO Box 142, Surfers Paradise, Qld., 4217, Australia. www.laughingwaters.com.au

First published 2002

Author: Chantal Dunbar
Editor: Susan Whitehead
Food Photography: Chris Chen
Food Stylist: Kirsty Cassidy
Design & Pre-Press by: Sharon Serci, Ocean Graphics
Printed by: Everbest Printing Co Ltd, China

The ingredients and methods of recipes provided in this book have been simplified and altered to assist the reader and to aid with creative reproduction. They are not intended as an accurate representation of the true calibre of cuisine enjoyed at P&O Australian Resort restaurants or an example of the skills of participating chefs.

While every effort has been made to ensure that the information and recipes in this book are accurate and safe, the publisher cannot accept liability for any resulting injury, loss or damage to property.

Cover: "New Growth", Bedarra Island.
Photographer: Michael Curtis

National Library of Australia cataloguing-in-publication

Dunbar, Chantal, 1967- .
    Australia's natural treasures: with recipes from paradise.

    Includes index.
    ISBN 0 9581050 0 6.

    1. Resorts – Australia.  2. Australia – Description and
    travel.  3. Australia – Social life and customs.
    4. Australia – Pictorial works.  I. Whitehead, Susan, 1955- .
    II. Title.

919.4

# contents

# introduction

Long ago, it is thought Australia formed part of the super-continent Gondwana. For many millions of years dense rainforest covered much of the land, but as the huge landmass broke apart and Australia began its slow journey northward, the climate became drier and only pockets of the vast rainforest remained.

Australia's dominant group of mammals, the marsupials, was among those most impacted by this dramatic environmental shift. Some adapted to suit their new habitats, while others met with extinction, hastened by the arrival of new predators across a land bridge from South-East Asia, and by the burning of large tracts of land by Australia's first inhabitants.

Evolution and history have left Australia a legacy of some of the world's most bizarre and wonderful creatures. They survived in this land of great contrasts where frozen highlands meet with temperate rainforest, and sunbaked desert and the depths of the Great Barrier Reef border wet, tropical jungle. But in the past 200 years alone, 17 of Australia's mammal species have become extinct, and a further 22 risk becoming casualties of human "progress", unless urgent action is taken.

In a book such as this, it's impossible to do more than outline what appears to have happened, although it is increasingly understood that if we are to continue to enjoy the diverse beauty of Australia's fragile environments, we must operate in a conscious collaboration with nature.

Through the lenses of some of Australia's most talented nature photographers, this book presents a glimpse of some of Australia's most distinctive sanctuaries for humankind and nature. Among them are places that have come to have special meaning: islands of turtles, birds, shipwrecks and tragedy, domains of enlightenment and rivers of shame. Each has a story to tell and most were plundered for their riches, but today they attract visitors who search for a different kind of treasure.

P&O Australian Resorts is the largest owner-operator of nature-based resorts in Australia, with a portfolio of seven exceptional properties located either within or adjacent to a National Park or World Heritage listed area. Early on in its stewardship of these pristine environments, the company realised that the beauty that attracts so many visitors every year could also put the environment at risk of being "loved to death".

By successfully balancing a continuous program of investment, upgrade and product development with an ongoing commitment to nurturing the precious wilderness environments in which these resorts are located, P&O Australian Resorts has carved the way for soft adventure tourism in Australia. Properties within the Australia's Natural Treasures portfolio include:

**Cradle Mountain Lodge:** a spectacular wilderness retreat at the gateway to the Cradle Mountain/Lake St. Clair National Park in North Western Tasmania.

**Heron Island:** a World Heritage listed coral cay fringed by the magnificence of the Great Barrier Reef itself, with a magical underwater world all its own.

**Brampton Island:** a lively island resort blessed with golden beaches and surrounded by a blue-water paradise, at the mouth of the beautiful Whitsunday Passage.

**Bedarra Island:** Australia's most exclusive island resort, located just off the tropical north Queensland coast, serves as an indulgent, private haven for no more than 16 couples at any one time.

**Dunk Island:** a tropical rainforest island resort offering a vast array of activities, Dunk is set within the Great Barrier Reef Marine Park, and three-quarters of the island itself is National Park.

**Silky Oaks Lodge:** a stylish resort on the banks of the Mossman River, Silky is surrounded by luxuriant rainforest and is located just a few steps from the ancient Daintree National Park.

**Lizard Island:** a remote, private paradise located near the outer edge of the Great Barrier Reef and boasting 24 pristine beaches, this premium property is "one of one".

At each resort guests are assured of finding every comfort. Understated but elegant quality accommodation is designed to complement, rather than compete with, the natural beauty of each unique location. Exceptional levels of dining and service play a significant part in the P&O experience. These form the essence of what has become the Australia's Natural Treasures portfolio.

Chapters within this book probe the secret pleasures you will find when visiting P&O properties. The resorts' chefs have shared some of their most cherished recipes and recommended some of Australia's finest boutique wines in the hope that when you leave the comforts of the lodge or resort, you will be able to re-create a little piece of paradise found.

I encourage you to use time wisely and explore the many natural treasures that Australia has to offer. And as you journey, allow your mind to wander through time, and consider the legacy your actions leave for the generations to come.

**Chantal Dunbar**

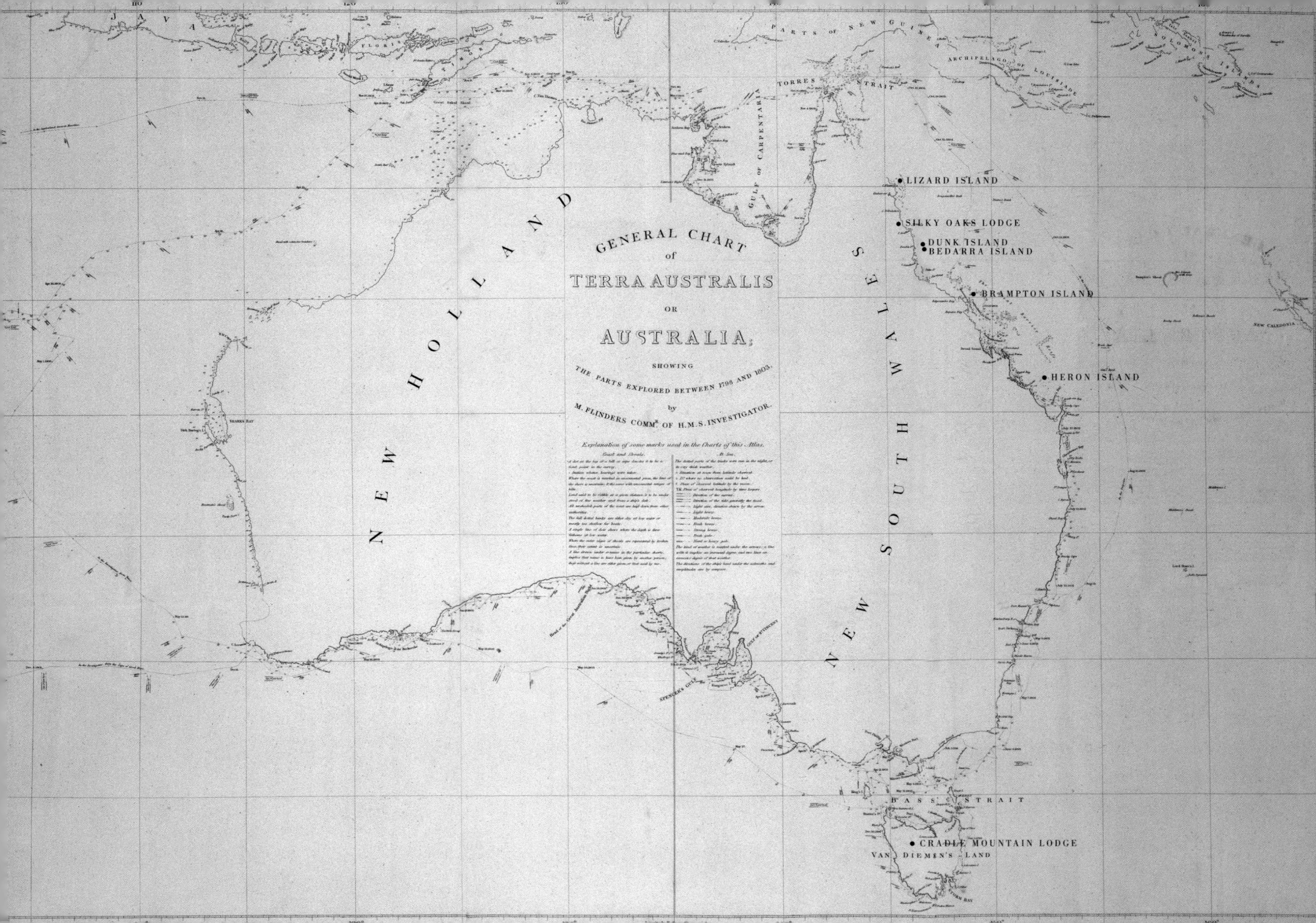

JAVA

PARTS OF NEW GUINEA

ARCHIPELAGO OF LOUISIADE

SOLOMON'S ISLANDS

TORRES STRAIT

GULF OF CARPENTARIA

NEW HOLLAND

NEW SOUTH WALES

NEW CALEDONIA

● LIZARD ISLAND

● SILKY OAKS LODGE

● DUNK ISLAND
● BEDARRA ISLAND

● BRAMPTON ISLAND

● HERON ISLAND

# GENERAL CHART
## of
# TERRA AUSTRALIS
### OR
# AUSTRALIA;
#### SHOWING
##### THE PARTS EXPLORED BETWEEN 1798 AND 1803,
###### by
###### M. FLINDERS COMMᴿ OF H.M.S. INVESTIGATOR.

Explanation of some marks used in the Charts of this Atlas.

SHARKS BAY

SPENCER'S GULF

GULF OF ST VINCENT

BASS' STRAIT

● CRADLE MOUNTAIN LODGE

VAN DIEMEN'S LAND

# a quick guide to australian wines

When Australian wines first stepped on to the world stage it was their difference that excited the market. Here were wines satiated with fruit, with an almost clinical purity that was so different from the restrained elegance and rustic characters of Old World wines.

Today the lines have blurred as French and Italian winemakers embrace the technological advances pioneered by Australia. Our winemakers have become more passionate about "terroir" (that wonderful French word that encompasses climate, soil, aspect, altitude and the myriad of influences on the humble grape), and the result is improved quality for wine-lovers the world over.

In global terms, the Australian wine industry is still in its infancy while it establishes which grape varieties are best suited to the country's burgeoning range of wine regions. But following is a quick guide to Australia's major grape varieties and the distinct styles that have evolved.

## SEMILLON

James Busby kick-started the Australian wine industry when he planted vineyards in the Hunter Valley in New South Wales in 1830. Since those early days the Hunter has produced a unique wine style – aged Semillon. When young, Semillon shows grassy, lemon flavours. It is picked early with consequent low alcohol (10 or 11 per cent) and receives no oak treatment. Over time it develops into a deep golden wine with rich, toasty, honeysuckle flavours. Wines such as Brokenwood Semillon, Mount Pleasant "Lovedale" and Tyrrells Vat 1 can cellar for over 20 years, building layers of complexity.

The youthful Semillons are perfect partners for soups, fish and seafood, while aged Hunter Semillons weave their magic with Asian-influenced or smokehouse meals.

## RIESLING

Australia produces a distinctive style of Riesling in the picturesque Clare and Eden valleys.

Situated two hours north of Adelaide in South Australia, wineries such as Grosset, Petaluma and Pikes produce Rieslings with heady aromas of lemon blossom, flavours of crushed limes and bone-dry, tongue-tingling finish.

These wines are a delightful match for seafood, salads and Thai or Vietnamese dishes. Riesling's racy acidity acts as a delicious counterpoint to flavours such as vinaigrette, olive oil, coriander and chili.

## SAUVIGNON BLANC

Australia and New Zealand may be keen rivals on the rugby field, but the New Zealanders are outright winners when it comes to Sauvignon Blanc. Wines such as Cloudy Bay Sauvignon Blanc have achieved an international cult following with their bracing intensity, passionfruit and gooseberry flavours and searing acidity.

The best Australian examples are from Lenswood in the Adelaide Hills (Geoff Weaver, Nepenthe). Lenswood is the coolest, wettest, highest wine region in South Australia – all conditions conducive to great Sauvignon Blanc.

In Margaret River in Western Australia, Sauvignon Blanc is blended with Semillon to add structure. Wines such as Cape Mentelle and Cullens Semillon Sauvignon Blanc blends are exceedingly popular wine-list items.

Fresh seafood, scallops, mussels and sushi all work well with goats cheese and Sauvignon Blanc, providing an alluring combination.

### CHARDONNAY

Chardonnay is a very compliant grape. It can be moulded in a variety of styles – austere and bone dry to plush and peachy, or rendered toasty and spicy with heavy vanillin oak character. The whole gamut is produced in Australia, but regions that excel are the cooler-climate regions of Adelaide Hills, Yarra Valley and Margaret River.

The Adelaide Hills Chardonnays are intense yet delicate, with white-peach flavours and a creamy finish. They are ideal with local crayfish and an Australian-style bouillabaisse.

Yarra Valley wines can be crisp and citrusy, while the Margaret River regions in Western Australia can produce wines of incredible concentration and finesse. Leeuwin Estate, Cape Mentelle and Cullen Chardonnays are shining examples. As well as the traditional food matches of lobster and chicken, these wines work well with white-mould cheeses.

### PINOT NOIR

This fussy, thin-skinned grape remains the most difficult to master. Only certain areas are suitable: cooler regions like Victoria's Mornington Peninsula, Yarra Valley and Geelong, as well as Tasmania. Pinot Noir smells of cherries, strawberries, mushrooms, and an exotic range of spices. Bannockburn from Geelong produces pinots of great intensity and length. The Yarra Valley's Coldstream Hills, Diamond Valley and Yarra Yering consistently produce

excellent Pinot Noir, as does Paringa Estate and Moorooduc on the Mornington Peninsula.

There is great interest in wines emanating from Tasmania as the popularity of Pinot Noir escalates. The classic food match is duck, but quail, rabbit and salmon dishes are all good reasons for a glass of Pinot.

### CABERNET SAUVIGNON

Almost halfway between Adelaide and Melbourne lies a strip of red soil over limestone. It is only 17km long and barely 2km wide. This is Coonawarra, which is famous for its superb Cabernet Sauvignon. Intense blackcurrant flavours with firm tannins and great length characterise Coonawarra Cabernet. The best makers include Bowen Estate Majella, Katnook and Wynns. Roast lamb teams beautifully, as does a piquant Australian cheddar.

Rivalling Coonawarra for Cabernet supremacy is the Margaret River region of Western Australia, which produces dark, dense, complex wines with extraordinary length. Cullen, Cape Mentelle and Moss Wood are among the best.

### SHIRAZ

Originally the workhorse grape for old-fashioned Fortified, Australian Shiraz is now at the peak of its popularity.

Australia's greatest wines, Penfold's 'Grange' and Henschke's 'Hill of Grace', are both made entirely of Shiraz. They are from the Barossa and Eden valleys of South Australia respectively. Along with McLaren Vale, these regions produce the quintessential blockbuster Australian Shiraz.

The peppery aroma and the opulent sweet plum and blackberry flavours are stunning. Rare eye fillet or venison fit neatly with this wine style.

Margaret River in the West produces a different Shiraz style – more savoury with cherry and spice and fine tannins. These are beguiling wines suited to grilled steak, spicy pizza or even game, and they are a treat with hard, crumbly cheeses.

This is not the full picture. We haven't mentioned Aussie Sparkling wine, Dessert wines or Fortifieds (including exquisite Muscats and Tokays), nor the exciting wines being made from more exotic varieties – Pinot Gris, Viognier, Sangiovese, Tempranillo and more. Hopefully we have whet your appetite to share our passion and discover Australia's many quality wines.

Previous page: Mist-shrouded Snow Gums at Waterfall Valley
Left: View across golden Button-grass moors to Cradle Mountain
Below: Tasmanian Devil
Right: The Autumn brilliance of Fagus

# visionaries

*" May your trails be crooked, winding, lonesome, dangerous, leading to the most amazing view. May your mountains rise into and above the clouds. "*

– Edward Abbey

"Spectacular," breathed Austrian immigrant Gustav Weindorfer as he gazed at the painted glacial tarns and marshlands spread out below him. It was 1910, and Weindorfer was standing on the windswept summit of Cradle Mountain amid a jumble of boulders and stunted alpine growth.

Embracing the grandeur before him, he instinctively spread his arms, making the now famous proclamation,

"There must be a National Park for the people for all time. It is magnificent, and people must know about it and enjoy it." Little did he know that this vision would shape the remaining years of his life and earn him a place in Australia's history.

Seven years earlier a meeting of like minds had taken place between the energetic botanist and fellow naturalist Kate Cowle. Their shared passion for the environment drew the pair together and, after their wedding in Kate's home town of Devonport, they decided to spend a five-week honeymoon camping on the slopes of Mt. Roland. There they explored the rugged landscape – Kate meticulously cataloguing the diverse flora and fauna that they encountered along the way.

It was then that they first saw the imposing peaks of Cradle Mountain, a sight so breathtaking that it drove Gustav to make the ascent and decide upon their future direction. Gustav became fixated with the notion of acquiring land on Cradle and, after raising sufficient funds, he was able to purchase a parcel of 400 acres.

By 1912 Waldheim, a home nestled among ancient Myrtle Beech and King Billy Pine, was built. The following summer the Weindorfers opened their doors for business and guests began to arrive. They proved to be the first of many willing to make the arduous journey and forego the comforts of home to experience the highland's magnificent wilds.

9

cradle mountain lodge

*Above: Gustav Weindorfer (seated) looking out towards Barn Bluff from the cairn on top of Cradle Mountain (January, 1911)*
*Right: The Weindorfers' tent near the northern end of Crater Lake (January, 1910)*

Soon, word of Cradle's dramatic beauty spread and Government officials, scientists and other distinguished guests came to stay at the forest chalet. Caught up in Gustav's enthusiasm to have Cradle Mountain officially recognised and protected, they used their wide-ranging influence to help the charismatic mountain man in the struggle to realise his dream.

Tragically, in 1914 Kate was erroneously diagnosed with "acute indigestion". She died two years later, with Gustav by her side, of what is now thought to have been breast cancer. The loss of his beloved wife – as well as the deaths of his mother, father and brother in the same year – shook Gustav to his very foundations. Although he continued to play host to guests at Waldheim, he spent long winters alone on the mountain, his only company a menagerie of animals that sought warmth by the chalet's fire. It was this solitary period, taken together with the xenophobic tendencies of wartime years, that earned him the reputation of being a hermit.

By 1921, it had become apparent that commercial exploitation threatened the area. Land was being cleared to make way for farms, and pressure to push deeper with logging was mounting. The effects of widespread trapping of animals were starting to show and, although Gustav harboured the fear that he would meet his end courtesy of one of the inquisitive Tasmanian Tigers that nosed around the chalet, he remained vehemently opposed to the Government-sanctioned culling of the species. Prompted by the ecologically devastating events that were unfolding around him, a heightened sense of urgency pushed Gustav to embark on a vigorous new campaign to secure official protection and recognition for Cradle Mountain.

Finally, on 16 May 1922, largely as a result of the efforts of Gustav, Kate and their friends, some 158,000 acres of land extending south from Cradle Mountain to Lake St. Clair were proclaimed a Scenic Reserve. Cradle Mountain was preserved for all time, and Gustav's dream was fulfilled 10 years before his death at the age of 58.

After Gustav died, Waldheim fell into disrepair and was subsequently demolished. But the public outcry over this loss was such that it has since been painstakingly rebuilt using the same methods originally employed to hand-split King Billy Pine into rough-hewn planks. Today, the chalet houses historical records from the period and is open to visitors to the Park. Every New Year's Day a memorial service is held there, to pay tribute to the vision and determination of an energetic Austrian and his dedicated wife.

The park now encompasses 161,000 hectares and has taken its place as part of the Tasmanian Wilderness World Heritage Area. Protecting Cradle Mountain's pristine wilderness is of critical importance in the battle to preserve what remains of Australia's natural heritage. Its haunting beauty serves as a reminder to all of what once was, and offers hope that man can preserve some part of his heritage for all our futures.

# bushwalkers' bliss

*SERVES: 2*

## INGREDIENTS

| | |
|---|---|
| 30ml | Kahlua |
| 30ml | Crème de Banana |
| 200ml | milk |
| 60ml | Baileys |
| 2 scoops | ice |

## METHOD

1   Blend all ingredients until smooth.
2   Sprinkle with grated chocolate.
3   Enjoy!

# gondwanan legacies

" *Even the most ardent botanist or geologist must pause to admire it with that silent outreach of the soul towards eternal beauty.* "

– Kate Weindorfer

Towering dolerite columns sculpted by titanic forces tell a story more than 100 million years old. The troughs of successive ice ages have gouged complicated drainage patterns into the landscape, their glacial debris channelling water into more than 4000 lakes and tarns. Cool-temperate rainforests of Celery-top Pine, Myrtle Beech and the majestic King Billy Pine bejewel their shores, providing shelter to some of the most strange and wondrous creatures to have evolved since Gondwanan times.

Tasmania is the most mountainous island on earth, and its snow cover is measured in metres for 3-4 months of the year. Its isolation has made it a final refuge for an extraordinary variety of species such as the Wedge-tailed Eagle, Black Cockatoo and rarely seen Pygmy Possum. Stands of ancient Huon Pine hold trees that are more than 3000 years old, but sadly, although one-third of Tasmania has been given National Park status, some 40,000 hectares of spectacular old-growth forest still remain open to logging.

The most visible of Tasmania's marsupials, the Common Brushtail Possum, can be seen foraging on open plains and in trees at night, and has no qualms about entering a cabin in the hope of adding variety to its diet. An agile climber, its furry tail is unable to support the weight of its chubby body, so it has developed opposable "thumbs" and clawless "big toes" to help it succeed in a variety of habitats.

One of Australia's most mythical mammals was the Tasmanian Tiger, or Thylacine. It is thought that this marsupial tiger-dog was displaced from the Australian mainland when South-East Asian seafarers introduced the dingo. Following European settlement of Tasmania, the Thylacine's tastes turned from wallaby to sheep – a habit that led directly to its disastrous fate.

Determined to protect flocks, the Government sanctioned a cull, which yielded more than 2000 Thylacine scalps between 1888 and 1908 alone. Any Tasmanian Tigers that remained were soon decimated by disease, introduced by farm dogs.

Although large tracts of Tasmania still remain inaccessible and unexplored, it is thought that the last Tasmanian Tiger died in 1936 in captivity in Hobart Zoo. Tragically this was the same year that a law was passed to make the Tasmanian Tiger a protected species.

*Above: The ever-curious Common Brushtail Possum*
*Left: Snow detail*

In the mountains the sun falls quickly, ushering in ice-chilled skies. Under cover of darkness nature-spotting is at its best: this is when one of the largest burrowing animals in the world, the Common Wombat, can be seen grazing the Button-grass moors. Wombats can dig up to two metres of burrow each night, and their underground corridors, which reach 30 metres in length and network with the burrows of other wombats, may be the work of several generations.

Despite their slow, lumbering manner, wombats can run at speeds of up to 40km/hour over short distances, but their general wariness of human contact and short-sighted demeanour have led observers to conclude – incorrectly – that this playful and intelligent marsupial is actually somewhat dim-witted and blind.

Nights are punctuated by the scuffles and screams of Tasmanian Devils as they emerge from their dens to scavenge along the roadsides. Each has a territory up to 20 hectares in size, but these often overlap, leading to regular confrontations during which the ears of the angry "devils" turn red as they growl and yell at each other over the carrion.

Another nocturnal feeder is the Quoll, which has all but disappeared from many areas of Australia, with the Eastern Quoll now found only in Tasmania. They are easily recognised by spots that run the entire length of their bodies, and can be seen dashing through the undergrowth, hunting for small mammals, birds, lizards and insects.

The female Quoll gives birth to as many as 30 young, each the size of a jellybean. With only six nipples to suckle from, those that fail to attach themselves quickly are left to perish, while the lucky ones remain in the pouch until they are eight to 10 weeks old. At this time, they climb on to their mother's back until they grow too big to be carried around.

The constantly humid air of the mountain provides nutrients to ancient coral lichen and encourages a thick, cushion-like covering of emerald moss that softens the tangle of roots and smothers quartzite boulders. As the early morning mist rises from the river, the elusive platypus can be seen chasing its final meal of the night, entirely unaware that Gondwanan times have passed, and its surreal world has ceased to exist elsewhere.

*recommended wine*

## LALLA GULLY
## SAUVIGNON BLANC

**Hailing from the Lalla Gully in the Piper River region of Tasmania, the elegant Lalla Gully Sauvignon Blanc teams beautifully with this hearty soup.**

# celery and pepperberry soup

## INGREDIENTS

| | |
|---|---|
| 1 | onion |
| 1 | clove garlic |
| 2 heads | celery |
| 2ltr | water |
| 50ml | vegetable oil |
| 500g | pepperberry cheese |
| | salt & pepper to taste |

## METHOD

1 Finely chop onion and garlic then fry in vegetable oil over a low heat until soft and translucent.

2 Roughly chop celery, add to the pan and add just enough water to cover the celery.

3 Bring to boil then allow to simmer for approximately 20 minutes.

4 Remove from heat and place in blender until a smooth, fine consistency is achieved.

5 Pass through a medium-sized strainer to remove celery fibres, and while soup is still hot crumble the pepperberry cheese into it, then blend again until smooth.

6 Return to the heat and bring back to the boil, seasoning with salt and pepper to taste.

7 Serve with freshly baked bread.

# seeking greater challenges

When Gustav Weindorfer dreamt of attracting people to Cradle Mountain, he couldn't possibly have known just how popular the area would become. Although close to a quarter of a million people now visit each year, its pristine environment and the palpable sense of isolation still remain as they were almost a century ago.

Today, a network of well-maintained, clearly signposted boardwalks allows visitors to pass over delicate ecosystems without negative impact. At the entrance to the National Park, the Visitor Information Centre houses an impressive selection of reading material and educational displays, providing insights to those who choose self-guided walks.

Short trails such as "The Waterfalls Walk" take in the splendid Pencil Pine Falls, where a permanent rainbow dances above the spray. Downstream, past stands of Myrtle Beech with tangerine-coloured fungi, the top of the Knyvet Falls can be seen. Here mossy embankments stand in frozen animation; icicles dangling from their overhangs; rivulets frozen mid-stream.

The circuit walk of Dove Lake passes secluded quartzite beaches that are perfect picnic spots, and offers stunning views of Cradle's jagged peaks above.

To see the lake from a different perspective, canoe trips can be arranged to cross Dove's placid waters and reach areas that would otherwise be inaccessible.

In autumn, 200-metre banks blazing red and orange with Fagus, the Park's only deciduous beech, contrast sharply with the vivid blue of icy-cold Crater Lake. On the shore, a boat shed built by the Weindorfers provides a welcome resting spot and a chance to enjoy a thermos of hot chocolate before returning to base.

Those who seek a greater challenge can embark on the famous six-day "Overland Track". This 80km hike starts near Waldheim in Cradle Valley and traverses south-east to Australia's deepest freshwater lake, the spectacular Lake St. Clair.

Those less energetic yet equally adventurous can try quad biking, horse riding or a scenic flight over the mountain. Night spotlighting of wildlife is another gentle activity during which some of Australia's rarest marsupials may be encountered in their natural habitat. From the comfort of a four-wheel drive, Pademelons, Wallabies, Possums, Wombats, Quolls and even Tasmanian Devils are likely to be seen, feeding under cover of darkness.

## TAMAR RIDGE
## CABERNET SAUVIGNON

Tamar Ridge winery is located in West Tamar near Launceston. The berry flavours and firm tannins of the Cabernet Sauvignon marry well with this combination of venison, field mushrooms and chestnuts.

recommended wine

# springfield loin of venison with drunken grapes

**accompanied by grilled field mushrooms, braised cabbage and glazed chestnuts**

## INGREDIENTS

| | |
|---|---|
| 600g | venison loin |
| 4 | large field mushrooms |
| 12 | chestnuts |
| 12 | black grapes |
| 1/2 head | red cabbage |
| 100g | apple |
| 250ml | red wine |
| 100ml | port wine |
| 250ml | brown stock |
| 100g | brown sugar |
| 50g | butter |
| 100ml | cream |
| 200ml | redcurrant jelly |
| 100ml | olive oil |
| | salt and cracked black pepper to taste |

## METHOD

1  Season venison with salt and pepper.
2  Seal each side in olive oil in a very hot frying pan then roast (200°C) until medium rare.
3  Warm port wine and plunge grapes in, allowing to sit for 40 minutes.
4  Thinly slice red cabbage, place with apple, redcurrant jelly and red wine in a saucepan and simmer for 40 minutes.
5  Caramelise shelled chestnuts in brown sugar, butter and cream until the mixture is smooth and syrupy in texture and chestnuts are well coated, then set aside.
6  Clean mushrooms, season with salt and pepper and sauté in oil.
7  Let venison rest for five minutes before serving.

### jus

1  Brown meat trimmings in roasting pan, remove grapes from port wine and deglaze.
2  Add brown stock and meat juices then reduce to desired consistency.

## TAMAR RIDGE PINOT NOIR

**Pinot Noir is the classic pairing for duck, and Tamar Ridge is one of Tasmania's best. This lovely wine exhibits spicy cherry flavours that give it a silky finish.**

# clover honey duckling

### with roast root vegetables, berry vinaigrette and cress salad

## INGREDIENTS

| | |
|---|---|
| 4 | duck breasts |
| 25ml | Tamar Valley clover honey |
| 150ml | olive oil |
| 1 | carrot (small) |
| 1 | beetroot |
| 1 | onion |
| 200g | pumpkin (peeled) |
| 1 | sweet potato (medium, peeled) |
| 150g | mesculin or cress lettuce |
| | salt and pepper to taste |

**vinaigrette** (makes 250 ml)

| | |
|---|---|
| 1 | small bunch spring onions or chives |
| 10ml | Dijon mustard |
| 1 punnet | raspberries |
| 200ml | olive oil |
| 50ml | red wine vinegar |
| | salt and pepper to taste |

## METHOD

1 Peel, slice and roast vegetables in oven (180°C) in olive oil.

2 Clean and score the skin of the duck breasts then season with salt, pepper and honey.

3 Place the breasts into a frying pan and quickly seal each side in hot olive oil until medium rare.

4 Remove from heat and allow to rest for 10 minutes before slicing.

### vinaigrette

1 Chop spring onion and crush raspberries.

2 Mix in mustard and whisk together with oil and vinegar.

3 Season to taste.

recommended wine

# rustic warmth

A wilderness retreat in the heart of Tasmania, Cradle Mountain Lodge rests beside the glassy calm of a well-stocked trout pond. The main Lodge exudes a rustic charm that glows with the warmth of half-a-dozen firesides, welcoming travellers in from the cold.

With a design reminiscent of an alpine village, guest cabins take in commanding views either of the pond or the valley below. The surrounding forest acts as a living museum, bringing nature literally to your doorstep, with possums appearing on verandas, and wombats grazing in the gardens.

Two of the most accessible National Park trails, situated on World Heritage listed land, wind their way right through the heart of the Lodge grounds. From hillside cabins the "Enchanted Trail" passes Pencil Pine River, offering a condensed display of the surrounding area's complexities. Overhead the tangled branches of Myrtle Beech filter the sun across mossy groundcover.

Frozen puddles decorated with intricate icy patterns lie scattered between clumps of Button-grass, and the rails of a bridge sparkle in the early morning light with a fringe of tiny white icicles.

The "King Billy Track" meanders through forest and past a 1500-year-old King Billy Pine. The silence here is broken only by the sounds of Bennett's Wallabies as they hop through emerald-green understorey startled by the presence of a human and give the impression that, somehow, you've mistakenly been transported back in time.

On Cradle, it's generally accepted that even if the sun is shining and the sky is clear, there is no guarantee that it won't be snowing in 20 minutes. To ensure that such extreme changes in weather don't detract from your stay, Cradle Mountain Lodge has gone to extraordinary lengths to provide a suite of modern comforts and conveniences that make a stay here delightfully memorable.

Enclosed fireplaces and down duvets ensure that night-times in Spa Suites are cosy. Distinct living areas are styled using contemporary Tasmanian furnishings, and huge spa baths provide welcome relief for muscles aching from unexpected use. But it's the little things that set Cradle Mountain Lodge apart; things that instil a feeling that it's a home away from home, from the private stash of home-baked cookies to the nightly canapés and a bottle of the smoothest of Tasmanian ports. Dragging yourself away from being so utterly spoilt is almost impossible.

With active days and early sunsets, the deep leather chairs of the Weindorfer Lounge beckon. This is the place to enjoy a good book, relax with friends, or simply prop up tired feet on an ottoman. The atmosphere is that of a private club: so strong is the sense of belonging that it confirms the spirit of Gustav Weindorfer remains alive and in good company here.

Tasmania has earnt a reputation for its fresh, locally-grown produce. Meals prepared in the Lodge's Highland Restaurant reflect the island State's four distinct seasons, and use ingredients that are typically unique to the region. A walk-in wine cellar is stocked with an impressive range of quality wines sourced from Tasmania's many excellent boutique vineyards. Guests are free to select a bottle to accompany their meal, or to enjoy a wine-tasting hour when they can learn about the island's winegrowing regions, and discover how it is that Tasmania also produces some of the finest cheeses in the world.

Each year Cradle Mountain Lodge hosts a series of "Taste of Tasmania" weekends that are fast becoming an institution. They run throughout July and August, and are designed to let guests enjoy a wide range of Tasmanian fare. Featuring cooking demonstrations, wine and food tastings as well as a number of guided National Park walks, the weekends ensure that participants leave the "food-fest" with a feeling that they have experienced the very best that Tasmania has to offer.

The National Park has many enchanting spots where you can stop for a picnic, and Cradle's scenic beauty provides a perfect excuse to suffuse the senses with a bottle of fine Tasmanian wine and a hearty gourmet lunch. Magical spots include Marion's Lookout with its 360-degree views, the pebbly beaches of Dove Lake, and the serene banks of Wombat Pool. Hampers can be ordered from the Lodge and include such delights as smoked salmon and cream cheese finger sandwiches, a selection of cold meats, crusty damper rolls, a chef's salad, cheese and crackers, apple juice and mouth-watering handmade Tasmanian fudge.

After a day of hiking the Lodge tempts with a "Mountain Herbal Soak". A touch of pure indulgence, a herbal footbath, is followed by a neck and shoulder massage and a lengthy foot massage. This treatment should be made compulsory for all who have been out exploring, as it rejuvenates the energy levels and soothes away aches and pains.

When evening falls, an informative slide show is presented at the Lodge by naturalist guides. It includes a briefing on the native flora and fauna and provides an opportunity for guests to learn more about the natural history of the area

One of the questions most often asked relates to the colour of the water. Its golden hue is the result of leached tannins from Button-grass and the Woolly Tea Tree. Another strange sight is the cream-coloured foam that collects at river bends and at the base of waterfalls. It is a natural derivative of the cutty grass plant, and it "softens" the water, making bathing a treat for the skin.

All water sourced from Pencil Pine River for use by the Lodge is first passed through UV and micropore filters as a precaution. Grey water is treated at an on-site plant and only eco-friendly soaps and detergents are used. Waste products are trucked off the mountain, with recyclable waste separated for processing. The chopped-wood supply found near the door of each cabin is sourced from forestry scrap on the North Coast, and mains power provides energy.

Ensuring that the environment remains pristine

requires the awareness and consideration of all who use it. This way, those who follow long after we have passed may still marvel at the splendours that we enjoy today.

# apple and sticky date pudding

**with icecream, toffee and vanilla bean sauce**

## INGREDIENTS

| | |
|---|---|
| 400g | dates |
| 400g | brown sugar |
| 60ml | water |
| 2 tsps | bicarbonate of soda |
| 170g | cold butter |
| 4 | eggs |
| 1kg | stewed apple |
| 400g | self-raising flour |

**toffee sauce** (makes 750ml)

| | |
|---|---|
| 125g | butter |
| 125g | brown sugar |
| 125g | golden syrup |
| 300ml | cream |
| 60ml | Butterscotch Schnapps |

**vanilla bean sauce** (makes 750ml)

| | |
|---|---|
| 1/2 ltr | milk |
| 120g | sugar |
| 1 tsp | vanilla essence |
| 5 | egg yolks |

## METHOD

1 Bring dates, sugar, water and bicarbonate of soda to the boil and simmer for five minutes.
2 Cream butter and eggs and add to the date mixture.
3 Incorporate the stewed apples and flour then pour into a well-greased baking dish, and bake (150°C) for 1 1/2 hours. Allow to cool.

**toffee sauce**

1 Bring butter, sugar and syrup to the boil, simmer until it turns into a soft-coloured caramel.
2 Remove from the heat and whisk in the cream.
3 Add Butterscotch Schnapps to taste.

**vanilla bean sauce**

1 Cream sugar and eggs.
2 Bring milk and vanilla to the boil and strain over the egg mixture.
3 Return mixture to the pot at a medium heat, stirring with a wooden spatula. Do NOT boil.
4 Cook until slightly thick and then remove from heat, place pot into cold water and stir until cooled.

## TO SERVE

When cool cut pudding into 12 cubes and reheat in microwave oven. Serve with toffee and vanilla bean sauce and a scoop of your favourite icecream.

*Thousands of tired, nerve-shaken, over-civilised people are beginning to find out that going to the mountains is going home; that wilderness is a necessity; and that mountain parks and reservations are useful not only as fountains of timber and irrigating rivers, but as fountains of life!*

– John Muir

*Right: View to Barn Bluff.*

Previous page: Schooling Yellowback Fusiliers
Far Left: Looking across the Wistari Reef to Heron Island
Below Left: Anemone fish
Right: Dive time

# what price paradise?

*In the end we will conserve only what we love, we will love only what we understand; and we will understand only what we have been taught.*

– Baba Dioum

The coral cay of Heron Island rests on a platform reef studded with numerous micro-atolls. It is part of the spectacular Great Barrier Reef, and was formed over many thousands of years as natural debris gradually collected on its leeward shores.

As the cay grew, winds, currents and migrating birds deposited a cocktail of seeds on its shores, the

hardiest of which germinated to form dense stands of Pisonia, Pandanus, Octopus Bush and Casuarina. The roots of these trees and shrubs stabilised the emergent cay and secured its future as a permanent island, which today shelters a bird community that's best described as "Manhattan-like" in its pace and density.

Heron Island is fascinating for anyone with even a remote interest in wildlife. An aquatic playground for divers and snorkellers, it is surrounded by a vast lagoon that boasts prolific coral growth of unparalleled beauty and 900 of the Great Barrier Reef's 1500 fish species. It is this aura of abundance that has earnt Heron a reputation as one of the most photographed and sought-after dive destinations in the world.

The area attracts a great many unusual sea creatures such as the giant manta ray, which boasts a wingspan of up to seven metres. Large numbers of herons, noddies and other seabirds crowd the tiny landmass. A rich migratory calendar sees bird numbers on the island swell to bursting point during the summer months when thousands of Mutton-birds descend on the already crowded cay.

At this time, Heron's beaches also become rookeries for nesting turtles, and from January to April the sands erupt with the arrival of thousands of their tiny hatchlings.

Above: Turtles at the Brisbane Fish Market (1935)
Right: When "eco-tourism" had a different meaning
(1938)

getting there:

A tiny coral cay with an area of just 18
hectares, Heron is one of the islands of
the Capricorn Group. Lying on the Tropic
of Capricorn, it is only 72km north-east of
Gladstone in the State of Queensland
and can be reached by taking a 30-
minute helicopter flight or a two-hour
launch trip from Gladstone.

Life was not always so idyllic here, as in times past,
Heron Island's natural riches endured a colourful
history of unimaginable environmental destruction.

First sighted by the crew of HMS *Fly* in 1843, the
island was given the name "Heron" by the ship's
geologist, Joseph Bette Jukes, who mistook the many
Egrets along the shoreline for Reef Herons.

In the years that followed, the reef was charted in
greater detail, and an influx of new settlers colonised
the Capricorn Coast. The sea's bounty attracted the
interest of fortune seekers who plied a prolific trade in
beche-de-mer, pearl shell and dugong meat. The
Capricorn Group of Islands grew in reputation as a
"virtually inexhaustible" supply of natural resources,
and commercial fishermen determined to exploit her
apparently endless supply of turtles soon targeted
Heron.

In 1923 the Australian Turtle Company was granted a
lease to establish a turtle-soup factory on the island.
The soup was destined for export to European
kitchens, and a haul of 2,500 turtles was forecast for
the factory's first year of operation. The turtle hunters
aggressively harvested mature turtles, with no
consideration for the sustainability of the resource, and
soon decimated the slow-breeding species. Indeed by
1927, the short-lived enterprise had succeeded in
stripping the area to such an extent that the company
voluntarily closed the factory because of the scarcity of
turtles.

Recognising the island's greater potential, Captain
Cristian Poulson took over the lease and started to
promote Heron as a fishing destination. In the early
days guests were accommodated in tents, but as time
went by the island became so popular with
holidaymakers that Poulson decided to shift its focus

to that of a resort, with fishing as the primary
attraction. He built cabins along the beachfront and
converted the old turtle-soup factory into a dining
room, kitchen and power plant. Then in September
1943, Heron Island gained official recognition for its
unique and beautiful environment when it was
declared a National Park.

On the evening of 28 November 1947 Captain Poulson
rowed his dinghy out to visit the launch *Irma*. After
sharing the location of his favourite fishing spots with
friends on board, he left to row back to Heron, but
was never seen again. Sometime later, his upturned
dinghy was sighted approximately four nautical miles
south of the island. What happened to Poulson
remains a mystery, as his body was never found.

Today the two turtle species that breed at Heron
continue to struggle along the road to recovery, with
the Loggerhead classed as endangered and the Green
listed as vulnerable. Their potential to recover from
past exploitation depends largely on careful
management of humankind's impact on the
environment, and protection of the food sources that
are critical to surviving populations.

# drop in the ocean

*SERVES 2*

## INGREDIENTS

| | |
|---|---|
| 30ml | Blue Curaçao |
| 30ml | Malibu |
| 30ml | Bacardi |
| dash | pineapple juice |

## METHOD

1 Build on ice, starting with the blue orange liqueur.

2 Add each of the other ingredients.

3 Top up with pineapple juice.

4 Enjoy!

# turtle time

Both Green and Loggerhead turtles can be seen around Heron's lagoonal reefs. Some of the turtles are resident here year-round but migrate to breed in other areas. Others may have travelled from as far away as Indonesia and New Caledonia, or from as close as Moreton and Hervey bays to nest on Heron's beaches. Climatic conditions determine the numbers that nest, but typically a peak is experienced two years after an El Niño event.

Using their flippers as shovels, female turtles crater the island's beaches during nesting season, digging large body pits before creating deep egg chambers by scooping sand away with their hind flippers. Into these they lay up to 120 ping-pong ball sized eggs in rapid succession. Afterwards the turtle fills in both pit and chamber with sand before lumbering back to the water, where they regain their freedom of movement. The entire exhausting process may take up to three hours to complete and is generally repeated several times in a season.

Eggs are not gender-determined when they are laid: rather, the warmth of the sand during incubation decides the gender, with cooler temperatures producing males. After six to 12 weeks the eggs begin to hatch, and a whole brood of hatchlings makes its way to the surface en masse. The tiny creatures take two to five days to dig up from their nests and, once

just under the surface, they wait until the cooling of night signals darkness, then all emerge in a rush.

Despite running the gauntlet of hungry seagulls, a high percentage of hatchlings actually makes it to the water, only to come to grief on the reef flat. Schools of sharks congregate in the shallows at dusk and make a fast meal out of the hatchlings. Those that make it past these opportunistic feeders then face years during which they must navigate a maze of environmental and man-made hazards.

Mystery surrounds the hatchlings' whereabouts during the first few years of life. It is thought they may drift with ocean currents, feeding on plankton near the surface, but sightings are rare, making this theory pure conjecture. What is known is that they reappear in shallow coastal waters when about five to 10 years of age and take up residence there for a time, growing at a rate of less than three centimetres a year.

There has been a dramatic decline in turtle populations over the last century. Understanding the extent to which commercial fishing, harvesting, pollution and an escalating human population cause human-related turtle deaths is critical, or one of the oldest and most fascinating of earth's inhabitants may cease to exist within our lifetime.

*Above: Pandanus fruit*
*Left: Green Turtle hatchling*

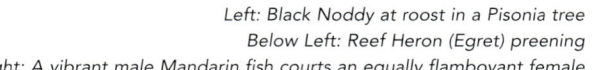

*Left: Black Noddy at roost in a Pisonia tree*
*Below Left: Reef Heron (Egret) preening*
*Right: A vibrant male Mandarin fish courts an equally flamboyant female*

More than 100,000 Black Noddies crowd branches and any other roughly horizontal surface throughout the island. They plant themselves on doorsteps and in the middle of pathways, and are seemingly oblivious to humans, who are forced to tread carefully so as not to step on them.

The Noddies' scientific name (*Anous minutes*) means small, silly bird. It was given to them in olden times, when they would foolishly choose the decks of passing ships as roosts, only to end up as a welcome change of diet for the sailors.

The spreading branches of the Pisonia tree are the birds' favourite home on the island, but once again their choice is unwise. During the nesting season the trees produce a resinous seed that sticks to the birds' feathers, and the Noddies' attempts to rid themselves of this excess baggage spreads the resin through their feathers until their tails can't fan open, and their wings stick to their bodies. Helpless, the crippled birds then flutter to the ground to await an untimely death from starvation.

In a comical nesting ritual, the female Black Noddy settles herself on a branch, watching as the male puts on an elaborate show by displaying as many as 90 apparently very similar leaves to her. She inspects each leaf from every angle before finally accepting one, which she places on the branch.

The raucous screeching and howling of thousands of Mutton-birds (Wedge-tailed Shearwaters), reuniting after a year apart, reaches a crescendo on Summer nights before some undisclosed signal brings it abruptly to an end. In times past mariners were convinced the island was haunted, as a chorus of the birds' wailing could be heard coming from the forest each night, sounding like the mourning of lost souls.

Each year the Mutton-birds return to the same nests, which consist of burrows in the sand up to three metres in length. They clean them out before laying a single egg in a chamber at the end. Here the egg incubates for some 50 days until hatching. Chicks are force-fed and quickly fattened before being abandoned to fend for themselves. Adult birds' poor takeoff and landing skills may be the result of learning to fly by pure trial and error with no parental guidance. Indeed Mutton-birds' disproportionately large wingspan makes them unable to alter course once committed, and they have been known to collide with trees, buildings and even people unfortunate enough to be on their flight paths.

## TAHBILK MARSANNE

**Tahbilk Marsanne comes from the historic winery in the Nagambie Lakes region of Victoria. With lemon flavours and crisp, dry finish it is a perfect partner to prawns, chili, lime and coriander.**

# spicy gulf king prawns

## INGREDIENTS

| | |
|---|---|
| ½ cup | crème fraiche |
| 1 tbsp | lime juice |
| 1 clove | garlic (chopped) |
| ½ tsp | dried chili flakes |
| 1 tbsp | coriander (finely chopped) |
| 2 tbsp | Joseph olive oil |
| 500g | large green prawns (peeled and deveined, leaving tails on) |
| 6 | Kipfler potatoes |
| 100g | baby spinach |
| 1 pinch | nutmeg |
| 80g | butter |
| 4 | lemon wedges |
| 2 | tomatoes (diced) |
| | sea salt to taste |

## METHOD

1 Combine crème fraiche, lime juice, garlic, chili, coriander and a pinch of sea salt in a large bowl, add prawns and mix gently to cover well. Refrigerate for 30 minutes.

2 Cut potatoes into five-millimetre rounds, brush with melted butter and grill for five minutes each side or until cooked and crisp.

3 Heat 1 tbsp. olive oil in a large pan and cook prawns in batches for 3-4 minutes.

4 Place the warm potatoes on a plate, sauté the spinach and season with a pinch of nutmeg and sea salt. Place on top of potatoes. Lay the prawns tails up.

5 Garnish with lemon wedges and the diced tomato.

# interactions with nature

 *Take nothing but photos, leave nothing but footprints.*

— Heron Island credo

Heron is a nature lovers paradise with reef-walking and relaxing with a cocktail the principal activities. A walk around the island on unbroken beach takes little more than 30 minutes, and on the way walkers will discover the magnificent Shark Bay, which is named after the harmless shovel-nosed rays (also called gummy sharks) that can be seen in the shallows. The bay's stunning width of white sand serves as an ideal picnic spot, and when winds ruffle the waters near the resort, calm seas can usually be found here.

Most of the 27 recognised dive sites take only five minutes to reach, so precious holiday time can be spent enjoying the 20-25m underwater visibility, rather than getting to and from dives. Adventure dives and night dives are available for experienced divers, and chartered day trips to nearby Wilson Island and the Wistari Reef can be arranged for those who wish to explore a little further afield.

If you've never been PADI certified, then Heron is the perfect place to enrol on a dive course. The beauty of the reef and warmth of the water make it easy for divers-in-training to relax and enjoy the new world that awaits their discovery.

The wreck of HMS *Protector* provides a point of particular interest in the small harbour channel, and spreading out from either side of it vast gardens of staghorn and plate corals are well-known resting spots for turtles and stingrays.

Equip yourself with mask, snorkel and fins, and jump in near the gantry in front of the resort to see large schools of Spangled Emperor and Parrot Fish, and of course the Damsels that hide between the fingers of coral outcrops.

At Heron it really is possible to walk straight off the beach and across reef-flats at low tide. Grab a spy-hole and walking stick from the Marine Parks Information Centre, then reef-walk out in front of the resort for a close-up look into rock pools that reflect another world.

The tides return, and so too do the many larger inhabitants of the reef-flats, causing the lagoon to once again pulse with life. This is the time to peer through the hull of the semi-sub as it glides across coral gardens and skirts the platform reef's outer edge. As the scene unfolds it is as though you are gazing into a fish tank of endless proportions. Guests have a chance to probe the vast knowledge of resort naturalists and, as they will tell you, it doesn't matter how often you venture out on to the reef, you're guaranteed to see something different every time.

## SANDALFORD VERDELHO

**Sandalford Verdelho from Western Australia has zingy, fruit salad characters that blend harmoniously with this lovely tropical chicken dish.**

# capricorn chicken

**with vegetable linguini and yoghurt sauce**

## INGREDIENTS

| | |
|---|---|
| 4 | chicken breast supreme (skin on, 250g each) |
| 40g | lemon pepper |
| 400ml | yoghurt |
| 40ml | vinegar |
| juice of 1 | lemon |
| 10g | crushed garlic |
| 10g | crushed ginger |
| 30g | Harissa paste |
| 30g | tomato powder |
| 20g | cumin powder |
| 10g | salt |
| 1/2 cup | coarsely chopped oregano |
| 2 | carrots |
| 2 | green zucchini |
| 2 | yellow zucchini |
| 4 | basil sprigs |
| 20g | butter |
| | salt and pepper to taste |

## METHOD

1 To create the sauce combine the yoghurt, vinegar, lemon juice, garlic, ginger, Harissa paste, tomato powder, ground cumin, salt and oregano.

2 Season chicken breasts with the lemon pepper and marinate in a small amount of the yoghurt sauce.

3 Seal chicken breasts in a small amount of olive oil, then cook in a pre-heated oven (180°C) for 6-8 minutes. Allow to rest for five minutes before slicing to serve.

4 Cut carrots and zucchini into thin strips (discarding the seeds of the zucchini).

5 Submerge vegetable strips in boiling water for one minute, then drain. Fold through soft butter and lightly season with salt and pepper.

## TO SERVE

Place vegetables on to plate. Arrange chicken slices on top. Drizzle sauce over and garnish with basil.

## GEOFF WEAVER CHARDONNAY

The combination of Mahi Mahi, sticky rice and coconut cream calls for an intense, complex Chardonnay, and Geoff Weaver from Lenswood in South Australia produces one of Australia's best.

recommended wine

# citrus spiked mahi mahi

**with lime sushi rice and coconut laksa sauce**

## INGREDIENTS

| | |
|---|---|
| 4 fillets | Mahi Mahi |
| | zest of one lemon |
| 1/2 tsp | lime oil |
| 500ml | water |
| 500g | sticky rice (short grain) |
| 1 tbsp | Laksa paste |
| 1/4 | onion |
| 100ml | cream |
| 1/2 can | coconut milk |
| 1/2 tbsp | sugar |
| 200ml | Sake (Japanese rice wine) |
| 2 | Kailan leaves (blanched) |
| 100g | Wakame seaweed salad (available from Japanese specialist stores) |
| 10g | red capsicum (diced) |
| 5g | sesame seeds (toasted) |
| 5g | black sesame seeds |

## METHOD

1 Rub Mahi Mahi in an even mixture of salt, pepper and lemon zest.

2 Place water, rice and lime oil in a pan. Bring to the boil, turn heat down to lowest point, place a lid on saucepan and simmer for 20 minutes.

3 In a pan sauté onion, add Laksa paste, cream and coconut milk, allow to reduce and thicken slightly, add sugar and Sake.

## TO SERVE

Place some of the steamed rice on to the serving plate. Lay some of the blanched Kailan on to the rice and layer the Mahi Mahi on top. Garnish with Wakame salad, diced capsicum and sesame seeds. Drizzle sauce around dish and serve.

# coral cay dreaming

" *Let the past drift away with the water.* "

– Japanese proverb

Heron has always been about giving guests the opportunity to immerse themselves in its extraordinary island and reef environment. From the time the launch departs Gladstone Marina, you feel that your adventure has begun.

Documentaries filmed at Heron and on the Great Barrier Reef are played during the two-hour journey, and it's not uncommon to see pods of Spinner and Bottlenose dolphins as the boat skims past deserted tropical cays.

Looming from the water at the entrance to Heron Island's harbour you will see the wreck of HMS *Protector*. Launched in England in 1884, she was

originally a South Australian navy ship that saw active service in the Boxer Rebellion in China, during World War I and also, when requisitioned by the US Navy for running supplies to

Papua New Guinea, during World War II. In her heyday, the *Protector* could out-steam and out-range *Nelson*, the flagship of the British Navy, but disaster struck in 1943 when she was holed by a tugboat and abandoned on Facing Island near Gladstone. There she remained until Captain Poulson raised the funds to purchase her hull. He floated her, then towed the wreck to Heron Island where she now forms an interesting breakwater and a valuable nesting place for the island's shy Black-naped Terns.

Looking out across an impossibly turquoise-coloured lagoon, the casual sophistication of the Pandanus Lounge offers a place to relax and take in the natural beauty of the reef. Day-trippers are not permitted to land at Heron, which ensures that the numbers of visitors at any one time are limited, and their impact on the island's delicate ecosystem carefully managed. Life is sweet here, with no crowds or noise pollution, giving Heron Island a wonderfully tranquil atmosphere.

The contemporary design of guest accommodation blends beautifully with the environment, reflecting the resort's sense of peace and uncluttered comfort.  A range of suites and rooms – many with panoramic views – makes Heron Island easily one of the best-value destinations on the Great Barrier Reef.

Mealtimes in the stylish Shearwater Restaurant are unpretentious. Ingredients are fresh, and whenever possible sourced locally to include the bounty of Australia's finest seafood. The weekly seafood buffet is considered a culinary highlight, and overflows with seasonal mud crabs, Moreton Bay bugs, whole-cooked reef fish, oysters and local prawns. Complementing the food is a showcase of Australian and New Zealand wines, favouring lighter styles such as Rieslings, Sauvignon Blancs and Pinot Noirs.

In 1951, the Great Barrier Reef Committee established a marine research station on Heron Island. Run by the University of Queensland, it is one of the best-equipped research stations in Australia, conducting numerous studies into the reef island environment and attracting marine biologists from around the world. Well-resourced with laboratories, aquariums, dive gear and boats, it can be visited as part of a tour from the resort.

The resort's Junior Ranger Program is specially designed to give kids from seven to 12 years an opportunity for some hands-on exploration of the island. During the turtle season they can help the turtle researchers with the Queensland Turtle Research Program, and as their knowledge of reef and forest ecology progresses, they can earn up to 15 colourful badges. Whether getting touchy-feely with a sea slug or learning about the coral cay environment, the kids are encouraged to log each day's discoveries in a fun workbook, giving them a lasting memento of their stay, and something to show their friends back home.

During turtle-breeding season, it's not uncommon to see staff and volunteers from the Queensland Parks and Wildlife Service, spotlights on their helmets, measuring and identity-tagging nesting turtles. This can provide a wonderful opportunity to take flash photographs of the turtles once they have entered a trance-like state during egg laying.

Some nights, it seems that all of the resort's guests are sneaking along the beach looking for a turtle. As they are not permitted to use torches, first attempts to locate the dark shapes of turtles are just as likely to result in guests patiently watching rocks and even other guests for long periods. Thankfully, resort naturalists tour the beach helping guests and educating them on best-practice for turtle spotting.

Although turtles on Heron Island have been known to wander on to paths and even to take a dip in the pool, they are most frequently seen on the stretches of sand on either side of Shark Bay. The sound of their digging can be heard under the Casuarina trees, and if you stay still long enough, you'll be able to watch them venture from the water and make their way up the beach to the high-tide mark.

Sunset and dusk are the best times to spot hatchlings, but lack of light presents a challenge, even though as many as 100 tiny turtles may scurry down the beach all at once. The hatchlings use light horizons to orient themselves with water, so artificial light from cabin verandas or flashlights can easily disorient them, resulting in a loss of precious energy that can mean the difference between life and death.

Considering guests' preoccupation with nature, it's hardly surprising that the resort operates a policy of zero impact on the environment. A desalination plant produces the required water supply, with grey water irrigating gardens that have been planted with cuttings taken from island natives, replicating the natural vegetation and growth seen in unspoilt spots like Shark Bay. Waste is sorted for recycling and shipped to the mainland for processing. Generators produce most of the required power, and water is predominantly heated by solar panels.

Nature presentations are held in the Wistari Room where interesting slide shows and documentaries are shown, and marine biologists from the Research Station occasionally discuss their findings with guests.

The Marine Parks Information Centre is a good place to chat with the resort's naturalists, leaf through their reference books and join them on interpretive nature walks across the island. These walks are a great way to learn about the traditional uses and medicinal benefits of plants found on the island, and present an opportunity to gain some insight into the birds' intrinsic link with the formation of the small coral cay.

You start to realise the hold Heron has on you when, as dawn creeps in on the horizon, you are still ranging the beaches and marvelling at how the sky has been so decadently painted with glittering stars.

# whole valencia orange almond torte

## INGREDIENTS

| | |
|---|---|
| 2 | oranges |
| 210g | sugar |
| 5 | eggs |
| 210g | almond meal |
| 10g | baking powder |
| 100g | mandarins with no pith |
| 60ml | vanilla bean icecream |

**orange sugar syrup**

| | |
|---|---|
| 100g | sugar |
| 100ml | orange juice |

## METHOD

1 Cut the oranges into small pieces, cover with water and a lid, cook until soft.  Whisk until pureed.

2 Whisk eggs and sugar until pale and fluffy, add the warm orange puree, fold in the almond meal and mix together thoroughly.

3 Lay in an individual well-greased flan tin and cook at 200°C for 20 minutes.

4 To make syrup, boil orange juice with sugar and then ladle over the cake once cooked, but still warm.

## TO SERVE

Un-mould the torte, and lay on a plate surrounded by the citrus syrup and slices of fresh mandarin.  Ball the icecream and arrange on top at the last minute.

Above: Wildlife at Heron Island

*... Nature's peace will flow into you as sunshine flows into trees. The winds will blow their freshness into you, and the storms their energy, while cares will drop off you like falling leaves.*

– John Muir

*Previous page: Grass trees in bloom above Oyster Bay*
*Left: Looking towards Carlisle Island from*
*Maryport Bay (the main resort beach)*

# the coconut isle

> " *Do not dwell on the past, do not dream*
>
> *of the future, concentrate the mind*
>
> *on the present moment.* "
>
> – Buddha

Fierce winds whipped at surging waters, sending waves crashing and clawing at the ironclad steamship as she sought shelter from the cyclone in February of 1883. Close to Carlisle Island conditions were so treacherous it was impossible to see land. But those on board the SS *Geelong* knew it was there; that safety – or fate – was only a matter of metres away.

Dawn broke on the new day, but the storm showed no signs of abating. The wind had shifted and the ship was dragging despite the crew's efforts to hold her with two more anchors. As she continued to founder, Captain Jenner became increasingly fearful for his passengers and crew, and in a desperate bid for safety he ran the ship aground.

Metal buckled, twisted and screeched as the ship hit Carlisle's rocky shore. She finally shuddered to a standstill, but the safety of the island was still well out of reach and the lifeboats were out of the question.

There was no choice but to get a lifeline ashore so that passengers and crew could use this to shimmy to safety. The Captain called for volunteers and, when no-one stepped forward, he took the line and plunged into the swirling waters, struggling with dogged determination until he reached the shore.

Although two of the crew were swept from the line, all others eventually found safety ashore and were rescued the next day by a passing ship. The captain received a medal for his bravery, but his vessel did not share in the good fortune. Unsalvageable, it was only a matter of weeks before she broke up along Carlisle's rocky north-west coast. Today only the bow of the wreck may be seen jutting unceremoniously from the dense forest, while a further 13 metres of keel lie flattened in just five metres of water.

61

*Above: Schooner at Maryport Bay (1950s)*

getting there:

Located at the entrance to the Whitsunday Passage, the Cumberland Group of islands is 32km north-east of Mackay, in Queensland. Access to Brampton is via Mackay.

It was due to the frequency of such shipwrecks that in the late 19th century the Queensland Government commenced a programme of introducing goats and coconut palms to coastal isles to provide a ready food supply for stranded sailors. Although few of these palm groves survived on surrounding islands, Brampton was the exception.

Brampton was used as a palm nursery until 1902, and the majestic coconut palms that decorated its protected bays became such a symbol that it was often referred to as the "Coconut Isle".

It was probably the island's comparatively fertile nature that prompted Joseph Busuttin and his brother Consiglio (Charles) to lease Brampton in 1916. They planned to breed chinchilla rabbits but, with the failure of that venture, they switched to breeding horses for the Indian Army. This exercise too was short-lived, thwarted by the advent of motorised transport.

The Busuttins' luck finally changed when, in the early 1930s, tourism in the nearby Whitsunday Islands started to gain widespread appeal. Brampton's coral sand beaches and lush forests made it easily one of the most beautiful islands in the Cumberland Group, so Joseph's sons set about developing its resort potential, building facilities so that in December of 1933 it was ready for its first guests. The cost of a three-week holiday, including steamer return from Sydney, was £27 at the time of opening.

In 1936, the island's beauty was formally recognised and Brampton was gazetted as a National Park. However, in recognition of the dedicated efforts of the Busuttin family, a special 20-year lease containing clauses to protect Brampton's National Park status was issued to Arthur Busuttin, who had taken up permanent residence on the island in 1934 with his wife, Jess.

World War II saw the closure of most resorts along the Great Barrier Reef and, from late 1942 to early 1943, the Secret Intelligence Service of Australia used Brampton and Carlisle islands as bases for their operations. Carlisle became a training-ground for Malaysian nationals learning how to infiltrate Japanese-occupied Indonesia to gather military intelligence to help Australia's war effort.

When the war ended refurbishments took place, the resort was reopened and visitors were once again able to enjoy Brampton's natural splendours.

Today some of the original coconut palms, now more than 100 years old, can still be seen, and Brampton's pristine shores remain a haven for those who go seeking sanctuary and replenishment.

# beach party

*SERVES 2*

## INGREDIENTS

| | |
|---|---|
| 60ml | mango liqueur |
| 60ml | banana liqueur |
| 240ml | pineapple juice |
| 120ml | coconut cream |
| 60ml | fresh cream |
| 2 scoops | ice |

## METHOD

1  Blend all ingredients until smooth.
2  Enjoy!

# pastel-coloured forests

With the exception of the resort area, Brampton and Carlisle have been National Parks since 1936 and 1938 respectively, providing sanctuary to a wide variety of flora and fauna, both native and introduced. The islands lie at the entrance to the Whitsunday Passage, joined at low tide by a sand bar that runs perpendicular to the airstrip.

The seabed slopes gently from Brampton's coastline, making the fringing reefs accessible, even to novice snorkellers. Despite its average depth of only two metres, Relief Point offers one of the island's best snorkel sites. Here you can find Brain Corals measuring 2-3 metres across, magnificent plate corals, and forests of pastel coloured Staghorn that attract Butterfly Fish and Damsel Fish, as well as a resident Maori Wrasse.

More than 60 species of birds are in evidence around the island, from the Wedge-tailed Eagle that soars high on thermals above Brampton's peak, to Australian Pelicans and noisy Sulphur-crested Cockatoos that frequent coastal areas.

Tall, symmetrical Hoop Pines thrive on Brampton's boulder-strewn hillsides. Found widely across eastern Australia, they are one of Queensland's most valuable softwood timbers and can be seen dominating the skyline and rocky headlands of Brampton's Turtle Bay. Once fallen, the wood of the Hoop Pine rapidly decays, leaving nothing but cylinders – or hoops – of bark, which give the tree its name.

Grass Trees, found on the ridgeline above Oyster Bay, are particularly well adapted to harsh conditions and able to withstand the fierce heat of bushfires. Known also as Black Boys, they are easily recognised by the dense tufts of spiky leaves that sprout from the tops of their tubular black trunks. A long, spear-shaped flower juts from their crowns, leading early European sailors to believe they were seeing spear-wielding Aborigines standing sentry on the hillside as their boats passed by.

Among the most ancient group of plants is the Macrozamia Palm, dating back more than 100 million years to the time of the dinosaurs. Part of a group of plants known collectively as cycads, their seeds contain a high starch content that traditional peoples ground into a flour after extensive leaching to remove the toxins. Painfully slow growers, Macrozamias take approximately 100 years to grow one metre in height – making some of the specimens on Brampton more than 4000 years old.

*Left: The crystal-clear waters of Oyster Bay*
*Above: Eastern Grey Kangaroo*

On Carlisle a beautiful 1000-year-old Melaleuca forest rests in a basin lined with basalt. One of the few plant species to have successfully adapted to having its roots submerged for prolonged periods of time, the Broadleaved Paperbark feels spongy to the touch and can store excess water for use in times of drought.

An eerie yellow light filters through the canopy and large clouds of dazzling blue and black Tiger Butterflies take flight before coming once again to rest on branches that bend and flex with the sheer weight of their numbers.

Green Tree Ants can be seen everywhere on Brampton and their nests are built in an intriguing fashion. The ants squirt ascorbic acid from their abdomens into the veins of leaves, which curl in response. Some of the ants then hold the leaves in place while others hold the larvae in their mandibles. They squeeze the larvae gently until a white silky thread is excreted from their mouths, then use this to weave back and forth, binding the leaves together. The result is a nest that may be as large as a football, and which forms a protective home that conceals the colony.

Gently knocking the nests brings the occupants scrambling outside to fend off the invader, and the ants can be picked up if you make sure to hold the head carefully between your thumb and forefinger to stop them biting. Licking the ant leaves your tongue with a slightly tingly sensation similar to that experienced from sucking a Vitamin C tablet. The taste is so popular in tropical north Queensland that the ants are farmed, and their abdomens are used to make jams, juice and sauces.

Walking through the forest the dense layer of leaf-litter cushions each step, creating the sensation of treading on a trampoline. In places it looks as though someone has been raking leaves into enormous mounds – some of which tower more than two metres high. This is in fact the work of the Scrub Fowl, a ground-dwelling bird that can be seen running through the understorey. They build the nest by scraping leaves together with their large orange feet and add or remove leaves each day to moderate the internal temperature to facilitate incubation of the eggs buried inside.

Koalas are native to the mainland, and none existed on Brampton prior to their introduction in the 1960s. Today, the descendants of these early settlers can occasionally be seen hugging their branches in the small Moreton Bay Ash forest near the resort's airstrip. They have been known to venture as far as the jetty, where one reportedly boarded the ferry to the mainland in a short-lived attempt to stow away.

Eastern Grey Kangaroos were also brought to the island in the 1960s. They can be seen in abundance grazing on lawns and adding an unusual dimension to the resort's small golf course. Having been on the island for so many years, they pay absolutely no heed to people and make an unusual sight with the impossibly long legs of a joey protruding from their pouches.

Emus were also introduced in the '60s, but they have gradually died out and the last remaining one, a cheeky pet named Yvonne, died in 1995, just days after the death of her owner.

## PIKES RIESLING

**Pikes Riesling from the Clare Valley in South Australia evokes crushed limes with a searing, racy finish. It works beautifully with crab and calamari.**

r e c o m m e n d e d   w i n e

# salad of blue swimmer crab and calamari

## INGREDIENTS

| | |
|---|---|
| 2 | blue swimmer crabs (cooked & cooled) |
| 2 | squid tubes (medium-sized calamari, trimmed & cleaned) |
| 10ml | sesame oil |
| 1 | Lebanese cucumber |
| 80g | bean sprouts |
| ¼ punnet | snow pea sprouts |
| 1 stick | celery |
| ¼ bunch | coriander |
| 3 | eschalots/spring onions |
| ½ | red onion |
| 8 sprigs | fresh mint |

## DRESSING

| | |
|---|---|
| 2 cloves | garlic |
| 1 knob | ginger |
| 1 | bird's eye chili |
| 30ml | light soy sauce |
| 15ml | sweet soy |
| 20ml | white vinegar |
| 20ml | peanut oil |
| | cracked black pepper (to taste) |

## METHOD

### seafood

1  Carefully remove legs from crab body and set aside.
2  Crack the crab body open and remove meat with a fork.
3  Cut calamari into small triangles and lightly score with a sharp knife.
4  Heat sesame oil in pan until smoking and add calamari, tossing constantly for one minute.
5  Remove calamari from pan and set aside.

### salad

1  Remove seeds from cucumber and cut into small batons.
2  Wash celery, remove leaves and cut in a similar style.
3  Cut spring onion on an angle and thinly slice red onion.
4  Toss all salad ingredients together.

## TO SERVE

In a small bowl, place crabmeat, calamari, salad ingredients and dressing. Position legs and claws next to the bowl.

# enjoy – don't endure

Some seek out sun-drenched isles in a bid to escape the hectic pace of everyday life. Their sole desire is a good book and a hammock slung between two palm trees. Others pass their days in windowless offices, unaware of the sun or the rain. A photo of a deserted palm-fringed beach pinned to the wall serves as a poignant reminder of a life they'd rather be living.

Brampton's ability to make people enjoy life, rather than endure it, is the perfect remedy for those needing to regain the thrill of being alive. With its extensive range of water sports and land-based activities, the choice of being flat-out busy or flat-out relaxed is yours to make.

Bushwalkers can explore the 7.7 square kilometres of the island by taking the 7km circuit track. Deviating to Brampton Peak, the island's highest point standing at 219m above sea level, your effort is well rewarded with panoramic views across calm waters to St. Bees, Keswick and the other Whitsunday islands.

Lapped by balmy waters, Brampton's gloriously uncrowded beaches and sheltered bays offer the perfect hideaway for an afternoon of seclusion. Guided by the resort's resident Marine Biologist, those interested in experiencing the marine environment will find a snorkel trip over fringing coral reefs to be a fascinating activity.

Jet-ski safaris and tubing definitely provide the most fun you can have sitting down, while free sailboard and catamaran sailing lessons are available most days on the beach. And yes – the endlessly patient water-sports staff will come out and get you if you forget how to turn around.

But if staying dry is the order of the day and you've never had the chance to play golf with a real kangaroo, then the resort's small chip 'n' putt golf course is the place to go for this uniquely Australian experience. Should 200 grazing kangaroos fail to sufficiently handicap, then a round of night golf – using glow-in-the-dark golf balls – will at the very least make the game amusing.

As the tide retreats and the sparkling coral shores are exposed, it's possible to beachcomb across to neighbouring Carlisle Island, where a gentle stroll through the Melaleuca Forest leads you to the remnants of the wreck of the SS *Geelong*.

Having tried your hand at archery, played a game of tennis or practised some beachside yoga, an evening hush finally descends upon the world. Those who are wise will enjoy a glass of wine, watch the sun as it dips behind the Whitsunday Islands, and take a moment to reflect on how life should always be.

## BOWEN ESTATE SHIRAZ

The Coonawarra region in South Australia produces some of the country's best reds and Bowen Estate Shiraz is a stunning example. Teamed with sirloin, the powerful pepper and plum flavours provide a wonderful balance.

# char-grilled sirloin

**with corn and red pepper salsa**

## INGREDIENTS

| | |
|---|---|
| 4 | sirloin steaks (each 180 gm) |
| 6 | sapphire or gourmet potatoes |
| 18 | rocket leaves |

### salsa

| | |
|---|---|
| 1 | corncob |
| 20g | butter (melted) |
| 1/2 | red capsicum |
| 1/2 | brown onion |
| 20ml | olive oil |
| | salt & pepper to taste |

## METHOD

1 Wash potatoes and bake in oven (180°C) for 20 minutes.
2 Husk corn and brush with melted butter.
3 Place corn on BBQ grill until each side is slightly blackened, then remove from heat and set aside.
4 Repeat process for capsicum.
5 When capsicum is fully blackened remove from BBQ and rinse under cold water until all the skin has washed off, then set aside.
6 Finely chop onion and capsicum and cut corn off cob.
7 Heat olive oil in pan until smoking and add salsa ingredients.
8 Cook for five minutes and season with salt and pepper.
9 BBQ the sirloin for 3-5 minutes each side or until cooked to preference.

## TO SERVE

Remove baked potatoes from oven, slice in half and place on plate with sirloin and rocket. Top with corn salsa.

## TAHBILK RIESLING

**This crisp, elegant Riesling from Nagambie Lakes in Victoria is a perfect match for the flavours of capsicum, chili and lemon.**

# vegetable skewers

**with peanut tabbouleh**

## INGREDIENTS

| | |
|---|---|
| 1 | eggplant |
| 1 | red capsicum |
| 1 | yellow capsicum |
| 1 | zucchini |
| 1/2 | red onion |
| 400g | long grain rice |
| 1ltr | water |
| 400ml | coconut milk |
| | salt & pepper to taste |

### tabbouleh

| | |
|---|---|
| 1 | bunch parsley |
| 2 | ripe tomatoes |
| 1/2 | red onion |
| 2 | cloves garlic |
| 80g | chopped, roasted, unsalted peanuts |
| 1 | medium hot chili |
| 20ml | olive oil |
| | juice of one lemon |

## METHOD

### skewers

1 Dice the eggplant and dust with salt to draw moisture out, then set aside for 20 minutes.
2 Dice the capsicum, zucchini and onion.
3 Wash salt off the eggplant before spiking all vegetables on to 12 skewers, alternating to achieve an attractive mix of colours and flavours.
4 BBQ until vegetables are lightly charred.

### rice

1 Wash the rice thoroughly.
2 Pour rice and water into a saucepan, seal with a well-fitted lid and cook over a medium heat for 25 minutes.
3 Fold coconut milk through rice.

### tabbouleh

1 Finely chop herbs, onion and garlic and dice tomatoes.
2 Add peanuts, olive oil and lemon juice.
3 Season to taste with salt and pepper.

## TO SERVE

Place a bed of rice on to each plate, then top with three skewers per plate and a generous serving of tabbouleh. Garnish with sliced red chili.

recommended wine

# the soothing beat

Upon arrival at Brampton Island, your first impression is likely to be one of surprise. For an island that is known for its broad range of action-packed activities, Brampton's a arming lack of crowds and noise contrasts sharply with any preconceptions you may have had.

If your vision of a paradise consists of uncrowded white sand beaches, soaring waters and magnificent coconut palms, then Brampton is sure to satisfy.

When arriving by air, your plane passes over the azure waters of the channel between Brampton and Carlisle. Blue-spotted rays can be seen gliding in the shallows, and an abundance of vacant deck chairs seem to have been positioned along the beach for perfect views of the sea.

An array of big kids' toys such as catamarans, jet-skis

and an aqua trampoline wait at the water's edge, beckoning you to come and remember how it feels to have fun. The resort's Beach Hut can provide snorkels and fins as well as a map of an underwater snorkel trail that shows you some of the most interesting aspects of the adjacent reef.

Spacious guest rooms take advantage of cool sea breezes and stunningly tranquil views. Although the rooms are air conditioned, screen doors make it possible to enjoy the warm nights and allow the gentle sound of the waves to lull you to sleep.

Jutting from the beachfront into the ocean, a uniquely shaped salt-water swimming pool is shaded by oversized umbrellas. A second, freshwater pool is located in the centre of the resort. Nearby, a massive fig tree acts as "camp" for large mobs of flying foxes. Their silhouettes can be seen as the ambient light drains from the sky.

The island was once a hunting ground for indigenous peoples who travelled from the mainland in flimsy bark canoes. Today, however, all flora and fauna are protected, offering those who might not otherwise seek an introduction to Australia's unique environment an opportunity to interact with the wildlife.

A great way to learn about nature's bio-diversity is to take a guided walk. Small groups explore the surrounding gardens, coves and hillsides, learning about Australian natural history and gaining insight into the island's environmental treasures.

wherever possible. This includes in-room products such as shampoo, as well as cleaning agents used in the resort kitchens and by the housekeepers.

All waste is transported back to the mainland for recycling or disposal, and the tertiary-standard sewage-treatment plant is designed to have a zero effect on the waters of the Great Barrier Reef.

Fresh water is a precious commodity on the island, and is produced by a desalination plant that was installed by P&O as part of its $8 million refurbishment programme when it purchased the resort in 1998.

All staff at the resort undergo an induction program in environmental protection and conservation, ensuring they are aware of and comply with the many environmental initiatives.

One such program is fish feeding, a popular activity at the resort that is carefully monitored by the Queensland Parks and Wildlife Service. Each morning guests are invited to climb aboard the miniature railway that runs along the coast and out to the deep-water jetty where a large gathering of fish enjoys a free brunch. Guests are discouraged from fish feeding outside of these times to prevent the fish from developing a greater reliance on this artificial food source, and to ensure that over-feeding does not occur, as this may cause aggressive behaviour.

Managing the resort's impact is not only restricted to nature. A range of treatments is available from the "Soothing Beat" spa, ensuring guests have every aid to help them unwind and get the most from their holiday.

Every year, thousands of visitors come to enjoy the sparkling waters, white coral beaches and delicate ecosystems that make up Brampton Island's National Park and Resort.

Because Brampton Island is home to such a diverse range of wildlife, the resort operates an environmentally friendly policy and works closely with the Queensland Parks and Wildlife Service to ensure its visitor impact is minimised.

In order to maintain this delicate balance with nature, the resort actively cultivates a respect and understanding of the environment among its guests, and recycled or biodegradable products are used

For the ultimate indulgence that will leave your body and mind feeling rejuvenated, a loofah body scrub using honey, sesame seed and coconut milk cleanses and promotes relaxation. This is followed by an herbal body wrap and special floral masque to nourish your hair, before being spoilt with a 45-minute aromatherapy-style massage using special essential oils.

No island stay is complete without a cocktail on the beach, but once each week Brampton Island goes a step further taking the restaurant outdoors to where a feast of a beach party is held under the coconut palms.

Attracted by the festivities, the curiosity of the island's kangaroos gets the better of them and they venture to the water's edge, hopping along the Main Beach foreshore. There they survey the goings-on of beachside diners, etching an unexpected memory that will remain long after the holiday is over.

As the hush of night descends on the island, the romantics at heart will be found sipping champagne as they cruise on the waters surrounding Brampton, watching the sunset as it casts its warm glow over the Whitsunday islands.

And for those with the stamina to fill every minute in this paradise, live entertainment will keep you dancing until bed, or a hammock, finally beckons.

recommended wine

## BROKENWOOD "JELKA" RIESLING

**From McLaren Vale in South Australia, Brokenwood "Jelka" Riesling is an intense yet subtle dessert wine with luscious mandarin flavours.**

# banana tarte tatin

## INGREDIENTS

| | |
|---|---|
| 2 sheets | ready-made puff pastry |
| 100ml | pure cream |
| 100ml | milk |
| 50gm | caster sugar |
| 1½ml | vanilla essence |
| 1 | egg |
| 20g | cornflour (sifted) |
| 30g | unsalted butter |
| 4 | ripe bananas |
| 20gm | brown sugar |
| pinch | cinnamon |
| 2 tbs | currants |
| 4 | scoops of your favourite icecream |
| 4 | sprigs mint leaves |

## METHOD

### base

1   Use a small saucer to press and cut four pastry rounds.
2   Place on an oven tray and set aside in the refrigerator.

### pastry cream

1   In a saucepan, slowly bring cream, milk, sugar and vanilla essence to the boil.
2   Remove from heat and whisk in the egg, followed by the cornflour.
3   Return to low heat and re-boil until thick.
4   Remove from heat and add butter.

## ASSEMBLY

1   Remove the tray with pastry rounds from the refrigerator and top each round with a little of the pastry cream.
2   Peel and slice banana and arrange on top of pastry cream.
3   Dust with brown sugar and cinnamon.
4   Bake in preheated oven (180°C) for eight minutes, or until golden brown.

## TO SERVE

Place each tatin on a separate plate, sprinkle with currants and top with a scoop of icecream. Garnish with mint.

*Most people dream of a tropic island, and at times yearn to get away from civilisation for the peace and beauty of an unspoiled paradise in the South Seas. In experiencing the beauty that is Brampton, that dream can truly be met – and comfortably surpassed.*

– Glenville Pike

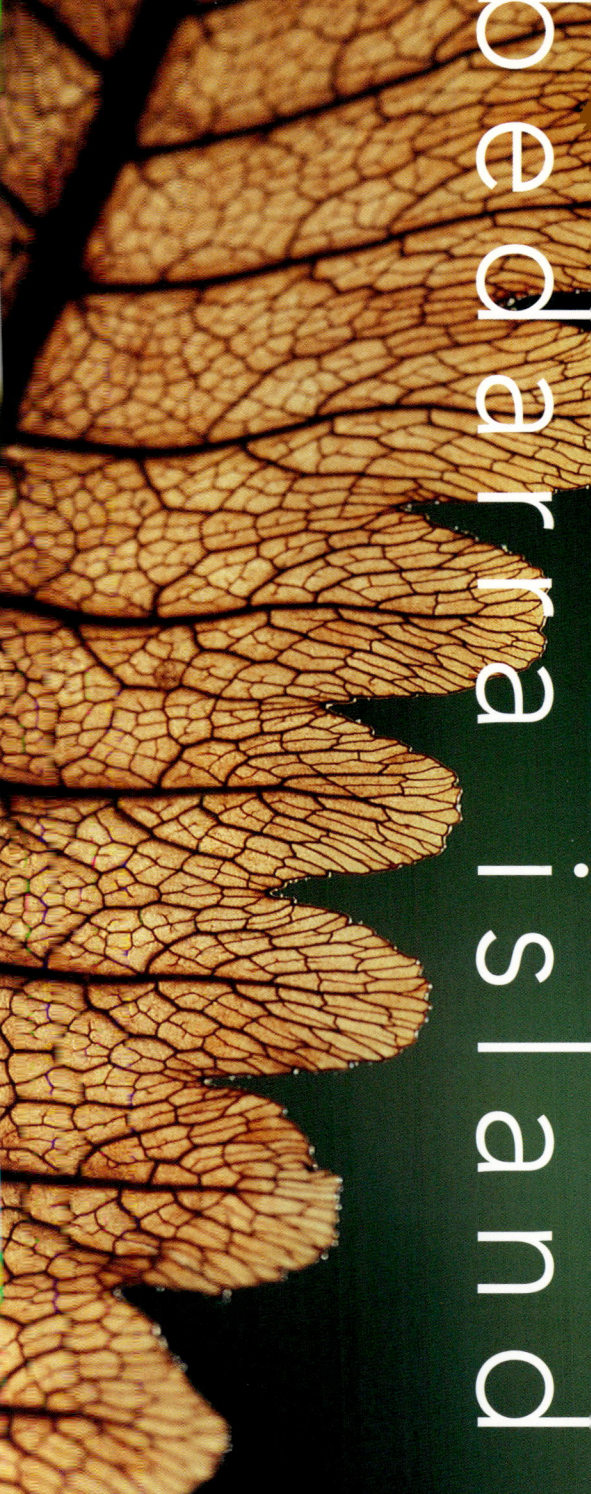

# deep-cushion comfort

*" A superb blend of the best of two worlds —*

*the one we know and the one we dream of. "*

— Bruce & Nikki Phillips (Bedarra Island Guest Book)

If you're looking for heaven on earth then Bedarra must surely be just one step short of it. Nestled in secluded Hernandia Bay, the Bedarra Island Resort looks out over the gentle curve of a white sandy beach to the glittering Coral Sea beyond. Not much has changed since Captain James Cook first sighted the island when his ship *Endeavour* made its historic voyage up Australia's eastern seaboard in 1770.

Lush tropical rainforest still spills from the island's untamed slopes and the seas abound with turtle and dugong. Pretty Bedarra, known as the Mother of the Family Islands, rests just a 30-minute boat ride from nearby Dunk, which Cook dubbed the Father. Around them, five more islands affectionately known as the Twins and Triplets decorate the waters. The seven islands share the common geographic characteristic of a spit of golden sand.

Bedarra has been known by no less than four different names. Indeed, it wasn't until early last century, when author E.J. Banfield was thought to have misconstrued

the Aboriginal pronunciation of Biagurra as "Bedarra", that a name finally stuck.

Although Cook is said to have sighted Aboriginal people on what is believed to have been Bedarra, the island is largely devoid of human habitation, save for the small, exclusive resort and an unobtrusive scattering of eight private houses at Doorilla Bay.

Over the years, Bedarra has attracted its fair share of romantics and interesting characters, among them an Englishman, Captain Henry Allason, who arrived in 1913 and sought Banfield's advice on a suitable island for purchase. Allason bought the whole of Bedarra as well as neighbouring Timana for the princely sum of £20, and he soon became famous locally for his long-distance swims between the two islands.

Unfortunately, the captain was called up for active duty in World War I after only a year on Bedarra, and was gassed in France. He survived, but spent his remaining years recuperating in Nice and never returned to his paradise in the South Seas.

Allason's investment proved sound, however, and in the 1920s he sold the island to Ivan Menzies for £500. Menzies' plan was to use Bedarra as a home for under-privileged English boys, but by 1934 his good intentions had come to nothing and the island was sold once again.

87

This was just the start of a long history in which Bedarra's fate was passed from hand to hand, but throughout and possibly in spite of the ambitions of all its owners, it has fortunately retained its natural rugged charm and unspoilt beauty.

No less than three of the islands within the Family Group became permanent residences for Australian artists, inspired by their wild, untamed terrain. Sporting little but a colourful sarong and wiry beard, Noel Wood was just the type of character you would expect to find on Bedarra. He and his wife Eleanor settled in picturesque Doorilla Bay in 1936 and lived on the island until 1993, when his parcel of land was subdivided, allowing the eight privately-owned houses to be built.

The remainder of Bedarra was developed into two separate resorts, the Bedarra Bay Resort and the Bedarra Hideaway Resort, which operated independently at either end of the island. In 1990 the north-western property, Bedarra Hideaway, was closed and the Bedarra Bay Resort was renamed the Bedarra Island Resort.

In March 1998, P&O Australian Resorts purchased all of Bedarra (except for the land originally owned by Noel Wood). Although the island is not deemed a National Park, management of the exclusive Bedarra Island Resort and the island itself is conducted according to standards of environmental best practice, as it is part of the Great Barrier Reef Marine Park.

The result is an island retreat that is intimate, private and unobtrusive in nature, attracting a clientele that seek the things money can't buy – peace, silence and time for contemplation.

## getting there:

Bedarra is located midway between Townsville and Cairns in Queensland, approximately five km offshore from Mission Beach. Access is by regular flights from Cairns to neighbouring Dunk Island, followed by a brief launch transfer.

# spliced papaya granita with midori

*SERVES: 4*

## INGREDIENTS

| | |
|---|---|
| 20ml | sugar syrup |
| 80g | ripe red papaya |
| 80ml | fresh mango juice |
| 40ml | Midori |
| 30ml | pure cream |

## METHOD

1 Blend sugar syrup, pawpaw and mango juice until smooth.
2 Pour into a shallow tray and freeze.
3 Pour Midori into four shot glasses, dividing equally.
4 Shave frozen granita with a fork and place on top of Midori.
5 Top with a little pouring cream.

# palm-shaded perfection

Bedarra's beauty seduces prominent guests from across the globe who come seeking an intimate haven surrounded by the rainforest's fierce tangle of green. You could hardly hope to find a more relaxed place to unwind than Bedarra, with its lush, tropical vegetation that spills onto the island's stunning white beaches.

Overgrown with an abundance of bougainvillea, hibiscus and palms, the island is a tapestry that appears to have been woven with time: nature helped only in part by the hand of man.

Three different types of epiphyte are prominent on Bedarra: the Staghorn, Basket Fern and Bird's Nest Fern. They grow on the trunks of towering palms and look for all the world as though they've been "planted" by an amorous gardener. The Staghorn's round, brown "nest" leaves act as big cups that catch water as it runs down the trunk of the palm. Bird droppings and leaf litter also collect inside the leaves, then decay into mulch that provides the plant with essential nutrients. The green antler-like leaves that give the fern its name photosynthesise and produce spores that are carried by the wind until they lodge in the bark of a nearby tree and another work of art is created.

A 45-minute walk through Bedarra's rainforest takes you on a winding trek to picturesque Hideaway Bay. At the very beginning of the trail the nest of an Orange-footed Scrub Fowl can be seen directly behind one of the resort villas. The birds are normally close by and are likely to startle you as they dart across the track, letting out an alarming call.

The trail ascends through seemingly impenetrable forest before levelling somewhat to follow the undulating ridge of the hill. It passes huge boulders that appear to have been stopped in mid-roll, precariously held in place by the tendrils of extremely strong vines.

Although there are scant glimpses of the ocean from the track itself, a number of detours will lead you to secret lookouts where deckchairs have considerately been placed to allow hikers to absorb the peaceful, spiritual quality of the rainforest in comfort.

When traversing the island, beware of the Wait-a-while Vine as it has developed a sinister way of reaching the canopy. The vines hook on to other plants with their long, barbed tendrils, using the sway of the breeze to help them climb towards the light. Only when they reach the canopy will the plants shed the spikes along their lower stems, so preventing animals (and people) from becoming inadvertently ensnared.

After cresting Allason's Hill, which is the island's highest point at 107 metres, the trail descends, past orchids clinging to lichen-encrusted rocks, to the revegetating site of the old Hideaway Resort. On the fringes of the forest you're likely to see the stunning Ulysses Butterfly, while panoramic views of mountainous Dunk and Bedarra's own long, golden sandspit can be enjoyed from the beach.

But it's Bedarra's seductive coastline with its excess of immense granite boulders that provides the most unusual vista for those fortunate enough to visit these shores. As continental islands, Bedarra and Dunk are the only two within the Family Group of Islands that can boast accredited fringe reef formations. Growing in relatively shallow waters, these reefs are extremely vulnerable to damage by storm-driven waves that can dislodge and crush corals that have taken decades to grow.

The waters around Bedarra are fertile feeding grounds for Green Turtles, which may often be seen resting on the surface just off shore. Dugongs have also been known to frequent these waters, but their numbers have steadily declined. These slow-moving creatures have few natural predators due to their size, and were once commonly seen in the waters around Australia. But over-hunting and the destruction of the beds of seagrass that they rely on for food has seen the dugong's name added to the endangered species list along with those of many other creatures.

# spicy green lentil dhal

**with papaya raita and char-grilled naan bread**

## INGREDIENTS

### naan bread

| | |
|---|---|
| 300g | plain flour |
| 1 tspn | baking powder |
| 1/2 tspn | bicarbonate of soda |
| 1 | egg (beaten) |
| 15ml | melted butter |
| 100g | yoghurt |
| 180ml | milk |
| | salt to taste |

### dhal

| | |
|---|---|
| 200g | green lentils |
| 600ml | boiling water |
| 4 tspns | cumin seed |
| 2 tspns | yellow mustard seeds |
| 30ml | olive oil |
| 1 | large brown onion (finely chopped) |
| 1 knob | fresh ginger (medium sized, crushed) |
| 4 cloves | garlic |
| 1 1/2 tbspn | curry powder |
| 500ml | hot water |
| 300g | ripe Roma tomatoes (roughly chopped) |
| 1 | cinnamon stick |
| 6 | cloves |
| 6 | cardamom pods |
| 1/4 bunch | fresh coriander |
| | salt & pepper to taste |

### raita

| | |
|---|---|
| 1/2 | Lebanese cucumber (seeds removed) |
| 100g | ripe red papaya |
| 100ml | sheep's milk yoghurt |
| 1/4 bunch | mint (chopped) |
| 2 cloves | garlic (crushed) |
| | cracked black pepper |
| | juice of 1 lime |

## METHOD

### naan bread

1 Sift together flour, baking powder, bicarbonate of soda and salt.
2 Add the beaten egg, butter, yoghurt and enough milk to form soft dough.
3 Cover with damp cloth and allow to stand in a warm area for two hours.
4 Knead on a well-floured bench for a few minutes before cutting into 12 even pieces and rolling with a rolling pin, until about 1/2 cm thick.
5 Brush with butter before cooking on a char grill or flat top (low heat) for approximately six minutes on each side, or until a light golden colour.

### dhal

1 Soak the lentils in boiling water for 15 minutes.
2 Warm the cumin and mustard seeds in a frying pan until aromatic and then grind with a mortar and pestle.
3 Gently fry the onion, garlic and ginger with dry spices and curry powder for 8-10 minutes.
4 Add the lentils (they will have absorbed the water), tomatoes, cinnamon, cloves, cardamom and hot water, simmer for 20 minutes.
5 Season to taste and fold through fresh coriander.
6 Roughly chop the cucumber and papaya, fold through yoghurt, mint, garlic, lime juice and pepper to taste.

## TO SERVE

Divide the dhal between the plates, with warm naan bread and a side of the yoghurt sauce.

# indulgence for the soul

Bedarra is the place to unwind and relax its natural beauty and serenity encourage guests to enjoy the island's innate sense of peace.

It is blessed with some of the Great Barrier Reef's most beautiful beaches, and there can be no better place to retreat into nature or enjoy time for reflection than one of its secluded coves. There are shallows to snorkel and places to sail but the indulgence of doing absolutely nothing generally holds the greatest attraction.

Most of the island's granite-strewn beaches are completely deserted and can be reached only by sea. The resort's small dinghies provide a convenient means of access and, as guests on Bedarra are restricted in number, it's unlikely anyone will encroach upon your private slice of paradise.

Many of the resort staff are keen fishermen and they're happy to share the location of Bedarra's best-stocked fishing holes with guests. Their one condition is that any fish under 40cm long are

immediately released back into the ocean to help ensure an ongoing bountiful supply. Recreational fishing equipment is available from the resort, and when you return the chef will prepare your catch and cook it according to your preference.

Located at Wedgerock Bay, you'll find dinghies, catamarans, sailboards and paddle skis for exploring the island's shoreline. Nearby, the Bedarra Beach House offers guests a gym, massage therapy room and lounge with Internet facilities. Its floor-to-ceiling plate-glass windows afford panoramic views across Wedgerock Bay, making the resort's gym easily one of the most scenic in Australia.

Private charters can pick guests up directly from Bedarra's jetty or day-trips may be joined by taking the resort's shuttle launch service to neighbouring Dunk Island. Serving as a convenient junction, Dunk's close proximity allows Bedarra's guests to join one of the many regularly scheduled day-trips for fishing or visiting the Great Barrier Reef.

## LALLA GULLY CHARDONNAY

**Lalla Gully from Piper's River in Tasmania is typical of cool-climate Chardonnay – full-bodied yet elegant. It works well with intense flavours, and the combination of Coral Trout, saffron potatoes and lobster salsa is perfect.**

# local coral trout

**with saffron potatoes, sugar snap peas and lobster salsa**

## INGREDIENTS

| | |
|---|---|
| 4 | coral trout fillets (skin on, no scales, 180g each) |
| 5 | southern gold (pink eye) potatoes (medium size) |
| 1 pinch | saffron |
| 120g | sugar snap peas |
| 60ml | clarified butter |
| | salt and pepper to taste |
| | sea salt |

### salsa

| | |
|---|---|
| 1 | medium lobster tail (cooked and cooled) |
| 2 | Roma tomatoes (ripe) |
| 1/2 | red onion |
| 1/4 bunch | chives |
| 15g | capers |
| 7 sprigs | parsley |
| 80ml | extra virgin olive oil |
| 15ml | fresh lime juice |
| | salt and pepper to taste |

## METHOD

### potatoes

1  Peel the potatoes then cut into three cm cubes.
2  Place potatoes in a pot, cover with water or stock and a generous pinch of saffron threads, blanch until soft.
3  Sautee the potatoes in clarified butter until just coloured.
4  Season and place on absorbent paper.
5  Blanch and season sugar snap peas with butter, salt and pepper.

### fish

1  Brush the fish with clarified butter, season with sea salt.
2  Heat an ovenproof, heavy-based pan over high heat.
3  Sear the fish until golden brown, turn and place in the oven for approximately seven minutes until cooked, yet still moist.

### salsa

1  Dice the lobster meat, tomato and red onion then place into a bowl.
2  Finely chop the chives and capers, and sprig the parsley.
3  Mix ingredients together, dress with the olive oil, lime juice, salt and pepper.

## TO SERVE

1  Divide potatoes and peas on plates evenly.
2  Place fish on top and dress with a generous amount of salsa.

recommended wine

## CAPE MENTELLE "TRINDERS" CABERNET MERLOT

Pork dishes marry beautifully with Cabernet Merlot blends and this one from Cape Mentelle in Margaret River, Western Australia, is a cracker. There are rich plum and mulberry flavours mellowed by toasty oak.

# roasted gungel farm pork

**with prosciutto, soft parmesan polenta and fennel vinaigrette**

## INGREDIENTS

| | |
|---|---|
| 4 | pork mini shoulder roasts (150g each)* |
| 4 pieces | prosciutto (thinly sliced) |
| 10 sprigs | thyme (finely chopped) |
| | cracked pepper |

### polenta

| | |
|---|---|
| 600ml | milk |
| 30g | unsalted butter |
| 150g | polenta (cornmeal) |
| 60g | parmesan (shaved) |
| | salt and pepper to taste |

### salad

| | |
|---|---|
| 1/2 bulb | baby fennel |
| 1/2 | red onion (medium) |
| 1 | red delicious apple |
| 1/4 bunch | chives |
| 10 sprigs | parsley |
| 60ml | extra virgin olive oil |
| 30ml | white wine vinegar |
| 1 tspn | caster sugar |
| | salt and pepper to taste |

*Suckling pig if available*

## METHOD

### pork

1 Roll the pork in cracked pepper and thyme, then wrap tightly in prosciutto.
2 Lightly sear the meat on all sides then cook in the oven (180°C) for eight minutes.

### salad

1 Lay the fennel thinly on to a flat tray, sprinkle with salt and allow to stand for half an hour.
2 Thinly slice the red onion into a bowl lengthways.
3 Cut the apple (wash but don't peel) into thin batons, chop chives into batons and sprig the parsley and add to mixture.
4 Wash the fennel (this should be lightly wilted) and add to the salad.
5 Dress with oil, vinegar and sugar then season.

### polenta

1 Bring half the milk and the butter to the boil.
2 Add the polenta, stir and lower the heat.
3 Cook for 20 minutes, stirring continuously and adding the remaining milk to keep a very soft consistency.
4 Once the polenta has lost its grainy texture, season with parmesan, salt and pepper.

## TO SERVE

1 Spoon a small amount of soft polenta on to each plate.
2 Cut the pork evenly in three pieces and place on top of the polenta.
3 Toss the salad and distribute evenly between all plates.

recommended wine

# resorting to nature

> *Sacred time is the collapse of the past and future into an eternal now.*
>
> – M. Kearl

Imagine a place where time is measured only by the passage of the sun. An island where only a fortunate few are allowed to savour the finer things that life has to offer. A private hideaway and exclusive haven that caters to those who desire a more civilised escape.

That's what the brochure promises and Bedarra doesn't let you down. Specialising in indulgence for the soul, the senses and the mind, it's a tropical island sanctuary that pampers guests with life's little luxuries and has a focus that's squarely on relaxation.

The intimate resort offers a hideout made possible

by its secluded location. It's hard to imagine a more laid-back pace than Bedarra, and wherever you look, the intense blues and greens of the landscape permeate and soothe your senses.

If what you desire is escape to an exquisite tropical isle where the hurried pace of life has been slowed right down, then simply leave the world to its own chaos and follow your heart here to reconnect with your inner self.

Bedarra combines breathtaking natural beauty with warm, friendly service and fine cuisine. It is one of only a handful of small island resorts in the world where a single investment in the self covers everything – from accommodation to gourmet meals, use of the bar and most activities.

Approaching Bedarra, the launch sweeps into gorgeous Hernandia Bay, where the only signs of the resort's existence are deck chairs that line the curve of the beach and a wooden feature deck stepping down to the shore.

The resort's 15 villas and central complex are all built below canopy level. They have been designed to blend with the natural environment and as such are totally concealed from view. Circular in plan, the central complex building was designed in 1987 by Byron Bay architect Christina Vadez and was inspired by two intertwined conch shells. The two sides of the building interlink by way of a central aperture, creating an effect of space and tropical harmony.

The architect explains that the guest villas were designed so that they seem to "grow out of the environment", and inside everything you could possibly need has been anticipated and provided for. There is a generosity of space that bestows a feeling of serenity and pampered comfort on their occupants.

Evidence of P&O's commitment to maintaining the resort's high standard of accommodation can be seen in the major refurbishments that were carried out in 1998 and 2001. The result; a feeling of luxurious tranquillity and decadent, simple beauty.

Sydney-based interior architects Pike Withers recently designed two ultra-elegant, privately-appointed pavilions that take Bedarra's hedonism to a whole new level. Set high upon the cliffs overlooking Wedgerock Bay, the pavilions are the epitome of understated elegance, with floor-to-ceiling glass, private plunge pools and extensive, free-flowing, indoor-outdoor living areas that embrace glorious ocean views.

Bedarra has several perennial springs oozing from storage basins in the granite bedrock, but these streams all reduce to a mere trickle during the summer months. They provide insufficient water to sustain the small resort, so a desalinisation plant was built in 1998. As at other P&O Australian Resorts, all waste is sorted for recycling before being shipped off the island to minimise man's impact on Bedarra's natural beauty.

The silence and feeling of tranquillity at Bedarra allow you to take stock and enjoy. Like everything else about this island hideaway, dining is a cherished experience.

Early evening at the resort is time for pre-dinner drinks at the legendary self-serve bar, which is stocked with a superb collection of fine wines, champagnes, beers, liqueurs and spirits. Cocktail books are provided for those wishing to try their hand at creating an exotic mix, and staff are never far away to offer their recommendations. If a cocktail is not to your liking, then why not try a glass of Bollinger Special Cuvée, the Bedarra signature champagne.

Dining on Bedarra is an indulgent yet sophisticated pleasure. Bedarra's talented chefs have a well-deserved reputation for creating inspirational dishes, and they change the menu each day to reflect the feel of the island and its guests. Only the very best produce, tropical fruits and boutique farmed meats are used to create a gourmet's delight, and the chefs are happy to indulge any special requests or dietary requirements that guests may have.

Back in your villa after dinner, an oil burner fills the room with the delicate aroma of Bedarra's signature scent. This has been specially blended to reflect the mystery of the island and is yet another of the small, yet personal touches that make a stay here so memorable.

On Bedarra they certainly know the meaning of the word service, and it is delivered in a warm and informal manner.

## BALLANDEAN LATE HARVEST SYLVANER

This dessert wine comes from the Granite Belt in Queensland. Its luscious, yet refreshing, clean finish perfectly suits fruit desserts.

# upside down tropical fruit sponge

## with mungalli double cream

### INGREDIENTS

#### sponge

| | |
|---|---|
| 100g | caster sugar |
| 3 | whole eggs |
| 100g | ground almonds |
| 40g | plain flour |
| 1/2 tspn | baking powder |
| 70g | butter (melted) |

#### fruit compote

| | |
|---|---|
| 50g | brown sugar |
| 50g | unsalted butter |
| 100g | pineapple |
| 100g | paw paw |
| 100g | banana |
| 1 | ripe guava |

| | |
|---|---|
| 200g | Mungalli double cream to serve |

### METHOD

#### compote

1  Over a moderate heat dissolve the brown sugar in the butter.
2  Add the fruit and cook for a further two minutes.

#### moulds

1  Grease four 7cm soufflé moulds with butter then dust with caster sugar.
2  Evenly distribute three-quarters of the compote into the bottom of the four moulds.

#### sponge

1  In a food processor, mix the sugar, eggs and almond meal at high speed until light and fluffy.
2  Fold through the flour, baking powder and butter.
3  Pour the sponge mixture evenly into individual moulds up to three-quarters full.
4  Bake (180°C) for 30 minutes.

### TO SERVE

Using a knife, run around the edge of the mould before turning it out upside down. Top with extra fruit compote and a generous dollop of double cream.

*... if the day and night are such that you greet them with joy, and life emits a fragrance like flowers and sweet-scented herbs, is more elastic, more starry, more immortal – that is your success ...*

– E.J. Banfield,
*Confessions of a Beachcomber*

# the castaway

Previous page: Early morning at Palm Valley
Left: Dunk and the Family Group of Islands
Below: The Spa of Peace and Plenty
Right: The iridescent Ulysses Butterfly

> *Fertile and fruitful, set in the shiring sea abounding with dugong, turtle and all manner of fish; girt with reefs rough-cast with oysters; teeming with bird life, and little more than half-an-hour's canoe trip from the mainland.*

E.J. Banfield – *Confessions of a Beachcomber*

Edmund James Banfield took up permanent residence on Dunk Island in 1897, after being told he had just six months to live. He and his wife Bertha had fallen under Dunk's spell a year earlier, when camping on the island with friends. At that time Banfield was co-editor of the *Townsville Daily Bulletin*, but after years of overwork his health had suffered to such an extent that his doctor advised him to make a radical change to his lifestyle or face certain death within months. And so it was that they became Dunk's first European settlers and soon, the greatest proponents of its charms.

Once recovered from a bout of seasickness brought on by the four kilometres journey from the mainland, Banfield set to work constructing a temporary shelter while a suitable site for a house was identified and cleared. Within a month the island's charms had reignited Banfield's youthful vigour, and he set about felling trees and sawing wood into lengths. Before long, a rough hut of hand-split timber, corrugated iron, and even the jib boom of a boat that had washed up on the island, had been built.

Located on a slight rise back from the southern end of Brammo Bay, the hut would serve as the Banfields' home until a larger bungalow was completed some six years later.

113

Above: E.J. Banfield and his dog
Right: The Banfields' home on Dunk (September, 1935)

getting there:

Located only four kilometres off the coast of Mission Beach, midway between Cairns and Townsville in Queensland, daily flights operate to the island from Cairns. Launch transfers are also available from Clump Point Jetty, as are water-taxi transfers from Mission Beach.

The traditional owners of Dunk were from the Djiru Aboriginal tribe. They called the island "Coonanglebah", meaning Isle of Peace and Plenty. The Djiru had lived in significant numbers in the mainland's coastal region, but Banfield noted their displacement by European colonisation, and expressed particular concern over the establishment of "missions" into which the remaining Aborigines were herded.

Banfield had long regarded Aboriginal peoples with respect, and he soon struck up a friendship with Tom, a Djiru man. Tom initially agreed to help the Banfields establish themselves on Dunk, but soon decided to stay on longer. At first Tom's wife Nelly would canoe across from the mainland to visit him – she was described by Banfield as gliding "into the jungle like a frightened snake" – but she too warmed to the kindly beachcomber and his wife. She came to live with Tom on the island, where she busied herself helping Bertha with domestic duties.

Over time, the settlers cleared approximately four acres of land, and wrestled the elements to grow fruit and vegetables there. Cows, goats and horses were introduced and allowed to graze freely over the remaining 360 acres of leasehold land. Soon the little farm furnished an almost totally self-sufficient lifestyle, and days on the island took on a decidedly tranquil feel.

Inspired by the richness of the untamed rainforest, Banfield's original book, *Confessions of a Beachcomber*, published in 1908, earnt him a reputation as one of Australia's first conservationists and become a London bestseller. His writings meticulously recorded the island's flora and fauna and were written in a romantic style, attracting escapists from around the world.

Not long before his death, Banfield realised that if his haven were left unprotected from development, its growing popularity would put it at risk. He wrote: "… to dwell upon the future of Dunk Island as not the least conspicuous item in a great insular National Park – a park not to be improved by formal walks or set in order to straight lines but just a wilderness – its primitive features preserved; its excesses unrestrained; its waywardness unapologised for. In such a wilderness, the generations to come might wander, noting every detail as it was in Cook's day and for centuries to come."

In June 1923 Banfield died from appendicitis on his beloved island. Bertha survived him by 10 years, and when she died her ashes were interred along with her husband's remains. In her eulogy it was said that while "Banfield was the very spirit of the island, Mrs. Banfield was the heartbeat, the very soul of their idyllic existence".

Banfield's final book, *Last Leaves from Dunk Island*, was published posthumously. His legacy and spirit are kept alive at one of Australia's largest and most popular island resorts and the beauty of Dunk remains very much as it was when it was first discovered by Cook.

# mango tango

*SERVES: 2*

## INGREDIENTS

| | |
|---|---|
| 30ml | vodka |
| 30ml | Triple Sec |
| 30ml | mango liqueur |
| 240ml | mango pulp |
| 2 drops | Grenadine |
| 2 scoops | ice |

## METHOD

1 Pour a drop of Grenadine in bottom of glass.

2 In a blender, mix remaining ingredients together until smooth.

3 Pour cocktails into glasses and enjoy.

# a lush mosaic

Rising with a reckless perfection the north-eastern slopes of mountainous Dunk are blanketed in a dense profusion of tropical vegetation. They peak at 271 metres at the summit of Mt. Kootaloo, which affords a superb view of the Family Group of Islands.

Dunk Island is best known for its luxuriant tropical rainforest and alluring white beaches, but it is home to a dazzling variety of bird species, and is also the place where the Ulysses Butterfly was first noted. Three-quarters of the continental island is National Park, and its fringe-reef speckled waters fall within the Great Barrier Reef Marine Park's protection.

The green mosaic of the ancient rainforest conceals Aboriginal rock art in caves that are well hidden among a tangle of moisture-loving flora. Plant life here thrives in the humid conditions, and is well watered by torrential summer downpours that are common to the area. This creates perfect conditions for the Giant Tree Frog, which emerges on damp, warm nights to hunt for insects in the vine forests around creek banks and in temporary ponds. Recorded at lengths of up to 14 cm, the Giant Tree Frog's white lower lip distinguishes it from its smaller relative, the Green Tree Frog, and explains why it is often referred to as the White-lipped Tree Frog.

During the wet season, sheets of water rain down upon the island's predominantly clay slopes, washing nutrients through gullies dominated by majestic rainforest species. Here, the large buttress roots of trees such as the Mahogany extend across the rainforest floor, sucking in the rich mulch that collects on the surface in a layer 5-10cm deep.

Light filters through a breach in the forest canopy awakening seed banks of pioneer species that have lain dormant for decades, facilitating the speedy germination of trees more commonly found in drier environments. They rapidly outgrow the rainforest saplings, reaching to the canopy where their comparatively smaller spread of foliage still permits dappled sunlight to filter through to the trees below.

The lifespan of pioneer trees is significantly shorter than that of the slower-growing rainforest species, and the time comes when the intruders inevitably fall away to become a ready supply of nutrients for the now-established rainforest trees. This remarkable cycle of canopy restoration often takes more than a century to complete, and results in a wonderfully varied pattern of vegetation.

Left: Buttress roots in the rainforest
Above: Giant Tree Frog

*Left: Bracket fungi starting the recycling process*
*Below Left: New growth*
*Right: Turtle Creek, where Bruce Arthur's ashes were scattered*

The island's dense tropical rainforests and mangrove-fringed shorelines form wonderful habitats for native wildlife that can sometimes be seen at close quarters.

The forest provides shelter to some of Australia's largest snakes, the most common being the beautiful Amethystine Python. It kills prey such as birds, bats and frogs by coiling itself around its quarry and tightening its grip with each exhalation until the victim eventually suffocates.

The protected Ulysses Butterfly favours the Corkwood Tree for laying its eggs, and the Corkwood's leaves are its caterpillars' preferred diet. Once hatched, the butterfly's six months of life is spent in the sunny forest canopy and forest fringe, flying at an alarming speed on brilliant metallic blue and black wings that have been known to exceed 10cm in span.

Some 150 species of birds can be found on Dunk, among them the splendid Metallic Starling, which is one of the most important forest-seed dispersers. Its striking black plumage shines with iridescent purples and greens, which make a dramatic contrast with its bulging, blood-red eyes. Metallic Starlings migrate here from Papua New Guinea each August, arriving when the supply of fruits and nectar-rich flowers is at its most bountiful.

Other commonly-seen birds include the popular Yellow-bellied Sunbird, which hangs its delicate tear-shaped nest under the eaves of roofs and from vines suspended over walkways. Hovering like a hummingbird, it probes flowers with its slender bill in search of nectar. The Sunbirds' gaiety of nature and fine song once made them one of Banfield's favourites.

Dunk has no wallabies, kangaroos, possums or large mammals, but there are plenty of bats, lizards, melomies and echidnas, as well as a couple of introduced pests, such as feral pigs and cane toads.

The scourge of the mainland, Australia's only true toad has made its way to Dunk, and is now found in sizeable numbers all over the island. The cane toad, which can weigh up to 1.36kg and is totally unafraid of humans, was introduced into Australia in 1935 to control beetles in cane fields. Although only 102 of the toads were originally imported, they have spread like a plague across Queensland, south into New South Wales and into the Northern Territory.

The toads secrete a milky toxin from large glands on their shoulders, making them poisonous and potentially fatal to any of Australia's carnivorous animals, which mistake them for an easy meal or mouth them in play. Even their eggs and tadpoles pose a threat to many natives.

118

## CAPE MENTELLE SEMILLON SAUVIGNON

**Arguably the best of this blend, Cape Mentelle Semillon Sauvignon from Margaret River in Western Australia has intense passionfruit and gooseberry flavours that team delightfully with seafood.**

recommended wine

# cold smoked barramundi tian

**with avocado salsa, thai red papaya dressing and cajun prawn popcorn**

## INGREDIENTS

| | |
|---|---|
| 2 | tomatoes |
| 1/2 | onion |
| 2 | avocadoes |
| 1/4 bunch | coriander |
| 100ml | yoghurt |
| 1/2 clove | garlic |
| 8 | prawns (shelled) |
| 10ml | olive oil |
| 6 tbsp | crème fraiche |
| 2 | cucumbers |
| 100g | cold smoked barramundi |
| 4 tsp | dill |
| 40g | salmon caviar |
| | Cajun spice |
| | salt and pepper to taste |

**dressing** (makes 250ml)

| | |
|---|---|
| 1/2 | ripe red papaya |
| 1 | lime |
| 1 | chili |
| 40ml | rice vinegar |
| 100ml | olive oil |
| 50ml | riesling |

## METHOD

1 Cut the cheeks off the tomatoes and dice into 1/2 cm squares.

2 Chop the onion and avocadoes to the same size and combine together.

3 Add chopped coriander, yoghurt, garlic and lightly season.

4 Fold ingredients gently together and set aside.

5 Mince prawn meat to a fine paste.

6 Heat oil to a high temperature and place dollops (3/4 tsp) of prawn paste into hot oil.

7 Once the prawn has puffed out like popcorn, remove from oil, place on a paper towel and dust with Cajun spice.

**dressing**

1 Place all dressing ingredients together and blend until smooth.

## TO SERVE

Peel and thinly slice cucumber in layers on to plate, spooning avocado salsa on top. Layer cold smoked barramundi in slices on top, then place scoop of crème fraiche on the top with dill and salmon pearls. Drizzle dressing around plate and garnish with the prawn popcorn.

# spoilt for choice

Dunk Island has so many activities on offer that it's hard to decide what to do first.

Much of Dunk's beauty is captured within the National Park, which features over 13km of walking trails. These are the best way for the casual spectator or committed biologist to appreciate and explore Dunk's superb tropical rainforest.

A pilgrimage that most visitors make is the hike to the top of Mt. Kootaloo, which takes about one hour and requires a reasonable level of fitness. During World War II, the air force established a base on Dunk Island and constructed the trail up to the summit where they built a secret radar station, the remains of which can still be seen. The trail begins at Banfield's grave, after which it crosses a swing bridge, and enters into thick forest. A good selection of birdlife can usually be seen and heard during the hike, and the spectacular views across the Family Group of Islands from the lookout make the effort required well worth it.

A 40-minute stroll from the resort leads to Bruce Arthur's Artist Colony. Open to the public on Mondays and Thursdays, a selection of locally made crafts is available for purchase. The colony was forced in 1974 when Bruce, a former Olympic wrestler opted for a more simple, unencumbered life in the Family Group of Islands. He became an internationally renowned

weaver, his work reflecting the images and colours of the tropical paradise that surrounded him. Although Bruce died in 1998, his rainforest retreat remains a peaceful and eclectic world of colour and texture, thanks largely to the commitment of resident artist Suzi Kirk.

Dunk is a continental island and so patches of fringing reef suitable for snorkelling can be found off Coconut, Muggy Muggy and Naturist beaches. While snorkelling from these beaches is enjoyable, water clarity and the variety of marine life pale in comparison with those encountered on the outer reef. Day trips run from the resort to the Great Barrier Reef, an hour from the island.

Those wanting to explore nearby Purtaboi Island or one of Dunk's many beaches at their own pace, have the choice of self-guided cruising in a small aluminium boat, or silently skimming the surface by paddleski, sea kayak, windsurfer or catamaran.

Adrenalin junkies are also well catered for, with parasailing, jet-skiing, tube riding, skydiving and waterskiing among the activities guaranteed to leave you with a rush. And when you've finally had enough of being either above or below sea level, there are terrestrial activities such as archery, golf, horse riding, tennis and squash to help you unwind.

# sugarcane cured chicken supreme

**with wild ginger and prawn risotto**

## INGREDIENTS

| | |
|---|---|
| 4 | chicken breasts (wing bones attached) |
| 4cm piece | sugarcane* |
| 1/2 bunch | coriander (roots only) |
| 3 tsp | garlic |
| 200ml | yoghurt |
| 80ml | vinegar |
| 80ml | lemon juice |
| 40g | tomato sauce |
| 80ml | olive oil |
| 3 tsp | paprika |
| 3 tsp | cumin |
| 2 tsp | chili |
| 1 tsp | salt |
| 2 tsp | lemon zest |

### risotto

| | |
|---|---|
| 1 | onion |
| 1 knob | wild ginger (small size) |
| 400g | arborio rice |
| 50ml | olive oil |
| 2 lt | chicken stock |
| 6 | prawns (cooked & peeled) |
| 80g | parmesan |
| 2 | limes |
| 200g | broccolini |

*Lemon grass may be used as a substitute if sugarcane is unavailable*

## METHOD

1 Bruise the sugarcane with a meat mallet, chop coriander, garlic, and all other ingredients.
2 Marinate chicken for three hours to allow flavours to seep through.
3 Remove chicken from marinade and lightly seal both sides in frying pan.
4 Cook in moderate oven (180°C) for 10 minutes.

### risotto

1 Sauté onion, ginger and rice lightly in olive oil.
2 Slowly add pre-heated stock until rice has absorbed all moisture and is soft to the bite.
3 Fold in prawns and parmesan cheese.

## TO SERVE

Spoon risotto on to plates. Place lightly cooked broccolini on to risotto and then position the cooked chicken on top. Garnish plate with half a grilled lime.

## CORIOLE CHENIN BLANC

Coriole in McLaren Vale, South Australia, produces a crisp Chenin Blanc with a green apple taste and tingling finish that beautifully compliments the light flavours of smoked ocean trout.

# hot-smoked ocean trout linguini

**with asparagus, shaved parmesan and gremolata dressing**

## INGREDIENTS

| 2 bunches | asparagus |
|---|---|
| 300g | hot-smoked ocean trout |
| 300g | linguini |
| 10ml | olive oil |
| | fresh parmesan (shaved) |
| | cracked pepper to taste |

**dressing** (makes 150ml)

| 1/2 bunch | parsley |
|---|---|
| 2 | anchovies |
| 2 cloves | garlic |
| 60ml | extra virgin olive oil |
| | zest from one lemon |
| | juice of half a lemon |
| | salt & pepper to taste |

## METHOD

1 Simmer pasta in salted water until cooked but slightly firm.
2 Cool under cold running water and set aside.
3 Wash and trim asparagus to small batons. Set aside.
4 Heat oil in pan until smoking then add asparagus and toss lightly for 2-3 minutes.
5 Add pasta and flake through hot-smoked ocean trout.

**dressing**

1 In a food processor combine all ingredients (discarding stalks of herbs). Blend to a paste and season with salt and pepper to taste.

## TO SERVE

At the last minute, add the dressing to the pasta and finish with shaved parmesan.

recommended wine

# in balance with nature

> "If a June night could talk it would probably boast it invented romance."
>
> – Berri Williams

It doesn't matter what time of day you gaze across Brammo Bay's shimmering waters, they always look as if they are encrusted with millions of tiny diamonds. The air is filled with the scent of rare and exotic flowers: frangipani, jasmine and white ginger flourish in the resort's nurtured grounds with such vigour that even the rainforest appears defeated.

Set just back from Brammo Bay, the resort's airy Plantation Bar looks out upon graceful coconut palms and a golden sandy beach under an impossibly clear blue sky. A large pool takes pride of place parallel to the beachfront. From within its depths two giant Ulysses Butterflies seem to flutter and sway as the strokes of a swimmer send out ripples across the pool's glassy surface.

There's a sense of space and serenity that's stirring for a resort as large as this one. But the island's sheer size, its abundance of lovely beaches and choice of secret places ensures that guests can take pleasure in their tropical surroundings without unwanted distraction from crowds or noise.

Just offshore sits Purtaboi Island, which is an important nesting ground for seabirds. Purtaboi is one of the few islands in the area that has no rats, cats, feral pigs or dogs, and it is here that four different species of tern camouflage their eggs among the coral rubble on the beach. To ensure visitors to the island don't inadvertently step on the eggs, access to it is closed each year from October to April.

Year-round Dunk attracts a clientele that's made up predominantly of families, honeymooners, wedding parties and couples. Its well-equipped Kids' Club provides a fun and friendly place for children to make new friends, learn about the environment and give their parents a well-deserved break.

Kids' activities are run mornings and evenings seven days a week, with one of the most popular being a visit to the island's Coonanglebah Farm. This modern descendant of Banfield's little farm is now 150 acres of charming Australian bush. Once a week the Kids' Club attendees enjoy pony rides and help with feeding some of the most contented animals you're ever likely to see.

A junior nature watch program has the kids out and about exploring the environment, searching for creatures such as the Ulysses Butterfly, Short-beaked Echidna and Green Tree Frog.

Teens are separately catered for with organised activities such as boom netting and mountain biking, as well as pool competitions and night golf.

While the kids are happily occupied, there's no better time to visit the Spa of Peace and Plenty for a spot of self-indulgence. Capturing the essence of Dunk, the resort's spa has used the island's floral fragrances to enhance a sanctuary that blends harmoniously with the rainforest. Designed in a subtle Eastern style, an extensive selection of treatments is available here, with emphasis placed on rich tropical fruits and products from the sea.

Mermaid's Song is Dunk's signature treatment. It uses plant and marine extracts to provide the ultimate in exfoliation and relaxation. The body is renewed with a peel made of crushed pearls before Dead Sea salts and aromatic oils are applied. The body is then kissed with a cool tonal mist to seal in moisture before an aloe finishing milk is gently massaged into the skin.

Dining on Dunk is again about choice, with a selection of restaurants, all with superb locations and wonderful food. EJ's on the Deck is the place to go for al fresco dining near the pool, while BB's on the Beach makes the most of casual dining for those who simply can't bear to drag themselves from the sand and the sun. The signature eatery is the Beachcomber Restaurant, perfectly positioned so that guests may enjoy a pre-dinner drink in the Plantation Bar before wandering through for their meal.

As dusk approaches, a smattering of guests can usually be seen silently gathering along the beachfront. Drinking in the tranquil beauty of the seascape, there's a sense of quiet anticipation as the sun's rays fade and a velvety lilac hue reaches across the unruffled waters from Mission Beach to the Isle of Peace and Plenty.

# exotic fruit treasure chest

**with chantilly cream**

## INGREDIENTS

| | |
|---|---|
| 125g | butter |
| 125g | sugar |
| 40g | golden syrup |
| 60g | plain flour |
| 2 | ripe guavas |
| 2 | tamarillos |
| 2 | figs* |

*Alternative fruits may be used.

### mango and strawberry coulis

| | |
|---|---|
| 100g | unsweetened mango pulp |
| 1/2 punnet | ripe strawberries |
| 80g | sugar |
| 50ml | water |

### chantilly cream

| | |
|---|---|
| 100ml | pure cream |
| 20g | caster sugar |
| 5ml | vanilla essence |

## METHOD

1  Pre-heat oven to 190°C.
2  Cream together the butter and sugar, then continue to cream while adding the golden syrup.
3  When smooth, slowly add flour and mix to a smooth paste.
4  Use six small cereal boxes (each approx six cm wide by 12 cm long) as moulds.
5  Place a sheet of greaseproof paper on to two oven trays. Smear paste over paper to approximately one millimetre thickness then bake for 10 minutes.
6  Remove from oven and lay box on cooked paste, turning it over until all five sides are gently imprinted.
7  Cut around the outside of the larger imprint and fold the warm paste over the box. Repeat until all boxes are covered.
8  Set aside to cool.
9  When crisp, remove the boxes.
10  Wash fruit, remove stems and slice into quarters.

### mango and strawberry coulis

1  Bring sugar and water to boil in a small saucepan.
2  Puree mango in food processor adding half the sugar syrup until consistency is smooth.
3  Repeat steps 1 and 2 above with strawberries for strawberry coulis.

### chantilly cream

1  Whisk ingredients until light and fluffy and sugar has fully dissolved.

## TO SERVE

Half-fill treasure chest with chantilly cream. Place on a bed of coulis and carefully position fruit into treasure chest.

# the dreaming

> *For every tree you cut, plant a seed.*
>
> – Kuku Yalanji saying

At the beginning of time – the time of the Dreaming – when the world lay largely flat and unformed, Gudurr, the Rainbow Serpent, created the land. As he moved across his domain, his body formed valleys, mountains and rivers that the ancestors came to perfect. They filled the night sky with their campfires, and as they worked, each living entity became connected with the Dreamtime, from which all life sprang.

For more than 50,000 years, Australia's indigenous inhabitants existed in harmony with the land, nurturing each tree as a living spirit. Guided by nature's subtle nuances and Dreamtime legends, they timed their hunting and gathering in conscious collaboration with the seasons. The result was an ecologically sustainable balance in which they became as much a part of the environment as it was a part of them.

The untamed landscape of the wet tropics between modern-day Townsville and Cooktown was home to 16 distinct Aboriginal groups. Nature in her abundance provided them with weapons, shelter and medicine, while their Dreamtime legends taught them how to detoxify poisonous plants to make them suitable for eating.

The Kuku Yalanji rainforest people inhabited a tribal territory in the shadow of Mt Demi (Manjal Dimbi) that stretched from what is now Cooktown in the east, west to Chillagoe, and then back to Port Douglas in the south. Their single language distinguished them from other tribes, and they lived in a territorial, complex society, travelling their homelands extensively over 1500 years using a network of rainforest walking trails.

*Previous page: The bubbling waters of the Mossman River*
*Left: Aerial view of the Daintree River meandering through the rainforest*
*Above: Saltwater Crocodile*
*Right: Canopy of Fan Palms, Cooper Creek*

Above: Logging in the Wet Tropics (1890s)
Right: One of Richard Daintree's photos of an Aboriginal woman (1860s)

Legend has it that the good spirit Kubirri watched over the Kuku Yalanji from mist-covered mountains above the Mossman Gorge. Long ago, the evil spirit Wurrumbu attacked the tribe, and in retaliation Kubirri exacted a punishment that exiled Wurrumbu to a bluff, where he was turned to stone. To this very day, he can still be seen as a natural rock outcrop standing among the clouds.

The arrival of European settlers in the mid-19th century heralded in one of Australia's most shocking examples of ecological ruin. Having already stripped the south's Red Cedar resources bare, timber-getters pushed north into the Wet Tropics, driven by the prospect of getting rich quick from "Red Gold". Huge stands of lowland rainforest were cleared and replaced with vast sugarcane plantations. Trees more than 700 years old were felled deep in the rainforest, kilometres from logging trails, with scant thought given to retrieving them for processing. Those too difficult or costly to reclaim were simply left to rot where they lay. The scale of devastation to the rainforest, and its impact on the Kuku Yalanji people, was immense.

Pushing further into Kuku Yalanji homelands, the settlers destroyed ever-larger tracts of pristine rainforest, displacing the indigenous people and removing their only source of food. Social structures crumbled and hunger set in, leaving the Aborigines with little option but to work for the timber-getters in exchange for a ration of food and tobacco. It must have been soul-destroying for the Kuku Yalanji to witness the obliteration of rainforests that had once provided refuge for the spirits of their dead. Soon a bloody frontier war erupted, but the widely-dispersed groups of Aborigines were no match for the superior weaponry of the settlers.

In the space of some 20 years, the loggers had exhausted the Red Cedar supply and departed with their spoils. They left a grim legacy upon the land: intense hostilities between settlers and Aborigines continued into the mid 1900s, when State Police rounded up all remaining Kuku Yalanji and relocated them to "missions" outside of their tribal homelands. Children were forcibly removed from their parents and, as some were too young to remember their true identities, many never returned.

Today, Kuku Yalanji people are gradually returning to tribal land at the Mossman Gorge. They have become successful tour operators and custodians of the Daintree National Park, weaving their rich cultural heritage back into the area and providing advice on managing the land for an ecologically sustainable future.

## getting there:

Silky Oaks Lodge & Healing Waters Spa borders the Mossman River at the edge of the Daintree National Park. It can be easily reached by a scenic coastal drive taking only 20 minutes from Port Douglas or just over one hour north from Cairns.

# canefire

*SERVES: 2*

## INGREDIENTS

| | |
|---|---|
| 30ml | dark rum |
| 30ml | Bacardi |
| 60ml | Malibu |
| 200ml | mango juice |
| 200ml | pineapple juice |
| | dash of Grenadine |
| | ice |

## METHOD

1   Fill each glass with ice.
2   Pour in all ingredients.
3   Finish with a dash of Grenadine.

# green dinosaurs

Seldom has a tract of wilderness elicited more interest and debate among the Australian public than the Daintree. The Greater Daintree lies between Cairns and Cooktown and encompasses an area of roughly 900 square km, much of it inaccessible. With almost 87% of the Wet Tropics' endemic species found only in this region, it is a living archive of plant evolution on earth, boasting a scientific value disproportionate to its size.

The Daintree shelters a biological diversity of no less than 330 bird species, 150 reptile or amphibian species and 74 species of mammal. Of particular interest are the Daintree's many primitive flowering plants, or 'green dinosaurs", the pollens of which can be traced back 100 million years. The continuing survival of these extraordinary plants depends largely on the ongoing protection of the wet tropics, as the natural habitats of some of them are restricted to areas no larger than a football field.

Although Cape Tribulation National Park was gazetted in 1981 to protect some 17,000 hectares of lowland rainforest, the Queensland Government of the time was determined to push a road through from Cape Tribulation to Cooktown, and open the north to development.

Strong opposition to the scheme resulted in a blockade, which saw conservationists dig themselves into the ground, chain themselves to trees and embark on a media campaign to raise international awareness of the Daintree's plight. Despite their tireless efforts

the scheme went ahead, destroying some of the most scientifically important lowland rainforest in the area, and the road was officially opened in December 1984

This prompted the conservationists to seek a greater level of protection for North Queensland's rainforests, so they spearheaded a movement to have it inscribed on the Word Heritage List. Although the Commonwealth Government backed the application, the State Government vehemently opposed it, even going so far as to send a delegation to the World Heritage body in Brazil in an attempt to block the nomination. They failed, and in December 1988 the Wet Tropics finally took its rightful place as the oldest tropical rainforest on the World Heritage List.

In December 1989, the State Government was over-whelmingly defeated at the polls and a new Government was installed. They moved quickly to co-operate with the Commonwealth Government, and in 1994 the Daintree Rescue Package was established with $23 million of funding allocated to the four-year programme.

As privately-owned land was not included in the World Heritage listing, half of these funds were used in an ambitious "buy-back" scheme, while the remainder went towards the development of an environmentally sensitive infrastructure that would allow visitors access to the Daintree without causing degradation or damage to the forest.

*Left: A Green Tree Frog*
*Above: Larvae of a Cup Moth makes its way across a palm frond*

Despite their World Heritage listing, the Daintree lowlands remain under threat from settlement and the unsustainable use of forest remnants. Further resources, education and the ongoing commitment of government will be required if these threats are eventually to be overcome.

Nature's infinitely delicate balancing act has played out over many millions of years in the Daintree. This natural hothouse supports extensive biological communities, and many species have become so interdependent that they need each other for their continued survival.

Although lowland rainforest is typically leafy, producing litter in proportions of 10 tonnes per hectare, surprisingly little of this is seen on the ground, due to an exceptionally efficient recycling process that takes place on the rainforest floor. Fungi, crucial in softening the host tissue of branches and logs, begin the process, then worms and beetles burrow deep inside the decaying wood, feeding on rich humus. These in turn attract birds and Striped Possums, which break log remnants apart hunting for the well-fed grubs. Within a period of only 2-3 months the cycle is complete and the forest replenished with life-giving nutrients.

At the bases of many trees lie their decaying fruits, which serve as ready fodder for the Daintree's high concentration of birdlife, the most symbolic of which is the rare, flightless Southern Cassowary. The Cassowary stands about two metres tall and is considered one of the rainforest's keystone species. It is responsible for the dispersal of seeds from up to 100 different types of tree, but with disturbance and clearing of lowland rainforest, the Cassowary has diminished in numbers and become increasingly aloof.

On the Cassowary's head sits a "helmet" of foamy cartilage sheathed in a hard covering. It's unclear what purpose this helmet serves, but one possible explanation is that it offers the big birds some measure of protection as they barrel through the rainforest understorey. Although seldom encountered, Cassowaries should be treated with respect, as when a male is caring for his chicks his behaviour can be quite aggressive.

When most people think of the jungle, a never-ending tangle of vines or lianas springs to mind. Their loops and twists hang in suspended animation, spiralling around the trunks of trees that have long ago died and rotted away. Some, like the Wait-a-while, or Lawyer Vine, have needle-sharp barbs on their ropy stems, while others grow hooks from their leaves that latch on to surrounding trees and help haul the creepers aloft.

Opportunists in the extreme, Strangler Figs are mercenary in their competition for sunlight. Beginning life as seeds dropped by birds high in the canopy, Strangler Figs germinate, sending a single long tendril to the rainforest floor in search of essential nutrients. A maze of criss-crossed roots spreads out and grips the trunk of the host tree, then gradually fuses together over hundreds of years. The crown of the fig grows flat over that of the host tree, depriving it of crucial sunlight, and the host tree finally succumbs to this onslaught and dies, falling away to become part of the recycling process.

There's a feeling of being watched as you move through the rainforest and, on closer inspection, you'll often see the primeval Boyd's Forest Dragon perched on upright branches of the lichen-encrusted trees. These lizards rely on general inactivity to escape detection, and are camouflaged by their colouration and thorny silhouette. On sighting an intruder they may slowly circle around their branches, but they will seldom leave the spot they have chosen as a lookout for the day.

The rainforest is filled with a distinctive chorus of whistles and chirps from frogs that are more often heard than seen. But the Daintree has not escaped a curious trend that has seen frog numbers mysteriously plummet and, in some cases, frog populations have disappeared from an area altogether. From New Zealand to North America the pattern has been the same, moving northward across 3 continents at a rate of 100km per annum. Theories abound to explain the decline in frog numbers, most based on the knowledge that frogs are sensitive barometers of the earth's health and are acutely susceptible to change.

Top Left: Southern Cassowary
Bottom Left: Platypus
Below: Striped Possum
Far right: Boyd's Forest Dragon

## TALTARNI ROSÉ

**From the Pyrenees region of Victoria, Taltarni Rosé is made from Malbec grapes. It is a beautiful salmon colour with aromas of raspberries and blackcurrant and a dry, zesty freshness. Teamed with this salad of rare roast lamb it is the perfect tropical food match.**

# salad of rare roast lamb

**with marinated vegetables and goats cheese crostini**

## INGREDIENTS

| | |
|---|---|
| 2 | lamb rumps (150gm each) |
| 20ml | olive oil |
| | sea salt to taste |
| | cracked black pepper to taste |

**salad**

| | |
|---|---|
| 6 serves | mizuna lettuce |
| 3 | globe artichokes (marinated) |
| 3 | tomatoes |
| 30 | fresh broad beans |
| 8 | black olives (pitted) |
| 40ml | Balsamic vinegar |
| | sea salt to taste |
| | cracked black pepper to taste |

**crostini**

| | |
|---|---|
| 1 stick | French bread |
| 30ml | extra virgin olive oil |
| 40g | goats cheese (chevre) |

## METHOD

**salad**

1 Pick the stalks off the mizuna lettuce and wash well.
2 Slice the artichokes.
3 Cut the tomatoes into wedges and place them on an oven tray with a bed of rock salt. Roast at (80°C) for one hour.
4 Shell the broad beans then blanch them in boiling water for three minutes.
5 Refresh the blanched beans in ice water then slip off the pale-green outer skin so that only the vibrant-green inner bean remains.
6 Add olives to salad ingredients and toss.

**crostini**

1 Slice the bread stick thinly on an angle to make 12 slices.
2 Lay the slices in a single layer on a baking sheet, drizzle each slice with olive oil and bake until crisp.
3 Smear each slice with a small amount of goats cheese.

**lamb**

1 Season the lamb rump with salt and pepper
2 Heat the olive oil in a frying pan and seal lamb for approximately two minutes each side.

## TO SERVE

1 In a bowl toss a little olive oil, balsamic vinegar, salt and pepper through the salad.
2 Slice the lamb thinly against the grain, and add to the salad.
3 Serve salad sprinkled with cracked black pepper with a side of two crostini per person.

# walking back in time

There is much to see and do in the Daintree and the scenic Mossman Gorge is usually the first stop on the agenda. Just minutes from the township of Mossman, its picturesque walking trails weave through the rainforest, leading to freshwater swimming holes decorated with huge granite boulders. It's a popular place for picnics and bushwalking as crocodiles, which are known to inhabit the river just seven km downstream, find the waters here too cold for their liking.

The Gorge is also a hub for Kuku Yalanji society and a great many cultural activities are staged in the area. Small galleries feature distinctive Kuku Yalanji art, and casual, open discussion can be had with the elders, who generously share interesting personal anecdotes from their past.

To view the Daintree without benefit of the wisdom of the Kuku Yalanji would be to miss out on one of its most fascinating aspects. Their guided walks transport visitors on a journey of discovery, providing insight into their spiritual connection with the rainforest and the tumultuous history of their tribe.

The characteristic green parasols of Fan Palms shade a leisurely stroll at the stunning Marrdja Boardwalk at Noah Creek. Significant plant species are pointed out for their traditional uses as bush food, medicines and weapons, and the complex method for detoxifying the seed of the Cycad plant is explained.

Flying foxes and bats can be heard long before they're seen, hanging inverted above the mangroves. Another of the rainforest's keystone species, they gather in camps that may consist of several million individuals, their numbers giving them a sense of protection, as they are a favourite food of the Amethystine Python that can sometimes be spotted coiled in a nearby tree.

Everyone who visits the Daintree comes with the expectation of seeing a crocodile. Opportunistic feeders, crocodiles stalk their prey underwater, striking with lightning speed then dragging their victims below the surface to drown them with the "death roll". Silky Oaks runs Twilight Cruises for up to six people, and on these trips it's not uncommon for fish to literally leap out of the water into the safety of the boat to escape the jaws of a pursuing croc.

At Cape Tribulation, the unique combination of fringing coral reefs and jungle-clad mountains can be seen coming together in a visual spectacular of colours. A striking feature of the foliage here is the sharp demarcation between the rainforest and sclerophyll vegetation.

Most excursions in the Daintree are designed for day-trippers, although the wealth of information imparted during these tours leaves visitors with an increased appreciation for the environment and gives them an intriguing glimpse into Aboriginal culture.

*Left: Cape Tribulation*

149

## HENSCHKE "KEYNETON ESTATE"

The Henschke name is famous for great reds and "Keyneton Estate" is no exception. It is a blend of predominantly Shiraz with Cabernet Sauvignon and Merlot. Rich plum and blackberry flavours and soft tannins cry out for high-quality steak to accompany them.

# char-grilled angus beef tenderloin

**with warm bean cassoulet, potato wafer and red wine jus**

## INGREDIENTS

| | |
|---|---|
| 4 | eye fillet Angus beef steaks (200gm each) |
| 4 sprigs | rosemary |

**warm bean cassoulet**

| | |
|---|---|
| 1/2 | Spanish onion (finely diced) |
| 100g | borlotti beans |
| 100g | black eye beans |
| 4 | Roma tomatoes (deseeded & finely diced) |
| 75ml | tomato juice |
| 1 tbs | sage (finely chopped) |
| 1 tbs | lemon thyme (finely chopped) |
| 1 tbs | continental parsley (finely chopped) |
| 10ml | olive oil |
| | salt & pepper to taste |

**crispy potato wafer**

| | |
|---|---|
| 4 | potatoes (medium-sized) |
| 20ml | melted butter (allow to stand and discard the milky part, using only the clarified butter) |
| | salt & pepper to taste |

**red wine jus**

| | |
|---|---|
| 2 kg | veal bones (chopped) |
| 1 | brown onion (medium-sized) |
| 1 | carrot |
| 1 stick | leek |
| 1 stick | celery |
| 1 head | garlic |
| 150ml | dry red wine |
| 1 sprig | thyme |
| 1 | bay leaf |
| 20ml | vegetable oil |
| 2ltrs | chicken stock |

## METHOD

### bean cassoulet

1 Soak beans in warm water for one hour, then drain and set aside.
2 Sweat the onion in the olive oil until soft, add beans and cook for a further three minutes.
3 Add tomato juice and diced tomato and continue to cook until beans are soft.
4 Slowly reduce any excess moisture.
5 Add herbs and season to taste.

### potato wafer

1 Peel potatoes and slice wafer thin.
2 Line a baking sheet with silicone paper and brush over a little of the butter.
3 Arrange the potato slices side by side on the baking sheet, slightly overlapping each other to create four circles.
4 Cover the inside of each circle with a few more potato slices. Brush with a little more butter and season to taste.
5 Bake in a preheated oven at 105°C, turning regularly for approximately one hour or until golden crisp.

### jus

1 Roast bones in oven until golden brown.
2 Finely chop onions, carrot, leek, celery and garlic.
3 Cook vegetables with olive oil in a pot at a high heat for 10 mins.
4 Add red wine and allow liquid to reduce by half.
5 Add chicken stock, thyme and bay leaf and reduce by two-thirds.
6 Strain and set aside.

### steak

1 Season meat with salt and pepper then barbeque or grill for approx three minutes each side.

## TO SERVE

Place the crisp potato wafer on the plate and top with warm cassoulet and beef. Pour on the jus and garnish with a fresh sprig of rosemary.

## TAMAR RIDGE SAUVIGNON BLANC

Tamar Ridge Sauvignon Blanc has intense passionfruit and gooseberry flavours with a crisp, zingy finish. The winery is based in West Tamar in Tasmania.

recommended wine

# bug tail ceviche

## INGREDIENTS

### marinade

| | |
|---|---|
| 250g | Moreton Bay bug tails (peeled) |
| 20g | coriander |
| 10g | fresh chili |
| 1 knob | ginger |
| 10g | palm sugar |
| 1 tsp | fish sauce |
| | juice of 2 fresh limes |
| | juice of 2 fresh lemons |

### dressing

| | |
|---|---|
| 1 | bird's eye chili |
| 1 clove | garlic |
| 25ml | sweet soy sauce |
| | half of the bug marinade |

### noodle salad

| | |
|---|---|
| 100g | fine glass noodles |
| 2 | tomatoes |
| 1/2 | small Spanish onion |
| 1 | spring onion stem (finely chopped) |
| 10 sprigs | fresh coriander |
| 20g | wood ear mushroom |
| 50g | papaya (diced) |

## METHOD

### bug tails & marinade

1  Finely slice bug tails and lay flat on a small tray.
2  Finely chop coriander, chili and ginger and add to the palm sugar, fish sauce, lemon and lime juices.
3  Pour half of the marinade over the bug tails.
4  Cover and marinate in the fridge for one hour.

### dressing

1  Finely chop chili and garlic.
2  Add sweet soy and leftover half of the marinade.

### noodle salad

1  Pour boiling water over the glass noodles.
2  Allow to stand for approximately 10-15 minutes, then rinse under cold water and chill.
3  Dice tomato and onion. Finely chop spring onion, coriander and mushrooms.
4  Add diced papaya.

## TO SERVE

Remove bug tails from marinade and gently toss them together with the salad ingredients. Place a neat pile of salad on to each plate and finish with dressing and coriander sprig.

*De la part de Laurent*
*Bon appetit*

# serenity

As the sun's first light strikes the mountaintops, the maniacal laughter of the Blue-winged Kookaburra rings out across the rainforest

Perched on the banks of the sacred Mossman River, the elegant Silky Oaks Lodge & Healing Waters Spa enjoys a location that's unique in the Daintree. Hemmed in on all sides by the oldest living rainforest on earth, the lodge has been designed in perfect harmony with its surrounds. A network of boardwalks winds through landscaped gardens blessed with an unfair profusion of flamboyant exotic blooms.

Here, deep in the rainforest, nature's artistic hand has created a tropical oasis where visitors can retreat from the pressures of an increasingly crazy world. Just 20 minutes from the restaurants, golf course and shops of Port Douglas, Silky's well-appointed treehouses blend unobtrusively into their surroundings. Furnishings are stylishly understated, creating a sense of space and harmony in private havens where CD players and spa baths combine a touch of luxury with pure indulgence

Extensive landscaping ensures seclusion and privacy for each treehouse. On the balconies hammocks are slung invitingly, allowing guests to kick back and enjoy the visual serenity that comes with being this close to nature.

In the main lodge building the "Jungle Perch" is a peaceful spot to sit and take in the changing moods of the rainforest. As the shafts of light in the sky meld into a warm afternoon glow, the chattering of cheeky Striped Possums can be heard announcing a changing of the guard, and the awakening of the nocturnal world.

Silky's open-sided Treehouse Restaurant looks down on to a river of tranquil calm. With its dramatic canopy position, the restaurant has become an icon among Tropical North Queensland dining locations. It is popular with diners from the lodge as well as from nearby Port Douglas, who come to experience its casual sophistication and meals that are inspired by the rainforest itself. Exotic ingredients are a feature of the light and luscious menu, which draws on the culinary influences of Asia and the Mediterranean to offer a modern Australian cuisine. Fresh, colourful and delicious dishes combine with the restaurant's unique setting to give diners an experience that would be difficult to match elsewhere.

155

In the wet season, tropical downpours cascade through the Mossman Gorge, altering the watercourse and flooding the many idyllic swimming holes. But during the cooler dry season the forest is at its best, with sprigs of tightly-bunched miniature orchids injecting an exquisite variation of shape and colour into the mass of green. A unique way to see the region is to take an early morning journey drifting across the Atherton Plains in the basket of a hot-air balloon.

You don't have to go far to experience the Daintree, as wildlife in the rainforest is distributed according to altitude, and there is an excellent variety of fauna to be found around Silky Oaks Lodge & Healing Waters Spa. One of the prettiest walking trails of the Mossman Gorge starts in the lodge grounds and continues up to the regenerating rainforest of Wave Rock. This area was once used as grazing land, so the canopy remains more open, which means it is less humid than Cape Tribulation. A few hundred metres past Wave Rock, the track ends abruptly at Fig Tree Rapids, where a deep swimming hole presents itself as the perfect place for a dip.

As most mammals in Australia are nocturnal, one of the best ways to see them is to take a night spotlighting tour with the lodge's Naturalist. The proximity of the lodge to the well-maintained trails of the Mossman Gorge allows guests to experience wildlife at its best. At night-time the forest becomes a hive of activity as Striped Possums leap from branch to branch, fireflies compete for brilliance with strange-glowing fungi and Leafy-tailed Geckos sit camouflaged on the trunks of trees.

Just below the Treehouse Restaurant, the Platypus Walk takes in narrow sand beaches that are touched by an unearthly softness of delicate ferns. Here, the Mossman River is clear like an aquarium, making it possible to see Catfish and Jungle Perch moving in the pebble-strewn shallows. There are canoes available for guests to explore the billabong and on the opposite bank, near a small waterfall the lodge's resident platypus can be seen at night, hunting for worms and small shrimp. The best time to see him is after a late meal, and as there are two loungers positioned perfectly on the riverbank, it is a superb place to come and reflect on the day.

The Healing Waters Spa offers a soothing retreat for those seeking to ease away the pressures of everyday life by pampering every nerve, muscle and bone in their bodies. The spa uses a range of natural Australian Aboriginal products, inspired by the sacred Mossman River and the ancient Daintree Rainforest, and drawing on extracts from rainforest botanicals such as Lillipilly, Cherry Alder, Lemon Myrtle, Tasmanian Kel, Wattleseed and Wild Rosella.

Reflecting the mood and culture of the environment, signature treatments such as "The Dreaming" promote a sense of emotional, physical and spiritual wellbeing. Included in this treatment is a desert salt exfoliation, mud wrap, Vichy shower, hair masque, facial and massage. Following such an intensive treatment your spiritual connection with nature is rekindled, and the

only decision left to make is whether to succumb to sleep or continue the indulgence with a glass of fine wine back in your spacious rainforest treehouse.

*Enjoy Rachiell*

## CLOUDY BAY
## LATE HARVEST RIESLING

**Cloudy Bay Winery in Marlborough in the South Island of New Zealand has received international recognition for the quality of its wines. This dessert wine shows apricot and honey blossom with a rich sweetness, balanced by a crisp acidic finish.**

# daintree tea and miracle fruit vacherin

## INGREDIENTS

### vacherin (meringue)

| | |
|---|---|
| 60g | egg white |
| 110g | caster sugar |
| 100g | icing sugar |
| 20g | cornflour |

### daintree tea sorbet

| | |
|---|---|
| 350ml | water |
| 150g | caster sugar |
| 50g | Daintree loose tea |
| | juice of 3 limes |
| 25g | miracle fruit berries (finely chopped) |
| 1 | egg white |

### thai red papaya consommé

| | |
|---|---|
| 200ml | water |
| 100g | caster sugar |
| 1 | stick of lemon grass (crushed) |
| 2 | Kaffir lime leaves |
| 150g | Thai red papaya flesh |
| | juice of 2 limes |
| | selection of fresh berries |

## METHOD

### vacherin

1 Whisk the egg white until soft peak stage, then add the sugar.
2 Keep whisking until the mixture has reached the stiff peak stage and is really smooth.
3 Add icing sugar and cornflour, and mix until smooth.
4 Pipe the meringue with a small, round nozzle in a round shape on silicone paper.
5 Bake at 120°C for approximately one hour, or until the meringue disc is crisp and dry.

### daintree tea sorbet

1 Bring the water and sugar to the boil in a pan.
2 Add the tea and allow to infuse until cool.
3 Strain through a fine-mesh chinois with cheesecloth.
4 Add the lime juice and the finely chopped berries.
5 Churn in an icecream machine and add the egg white when the sorbet is almost done.
6 Keep in the freezer.

### thai red papaya consommé

1 Bring the sugar and water to the boil in a pan with the lemon grass and lime leaves.
2 Allow to infuse while cooling down.
3 Strain through a fine chinois.
4 In a bar blender, blend the syrup with the papaya pulp and the lime juice.
5 Let drip overnight through cheesecloth.

## TO SERVE

Place one of the meringue discs at the bottom of a high ring or a mould matching its size. Pipe the sorbet on to it and top with another meringue disc. Serve in a bowl with fresh berries, lemon grass and Thai red papaya consommé.

*" … The earth does not belong to man; man belongs to the earth. This we know. All things are connected like the blood which unites one family. All things are connected. Whatever befalls the earth befalls the sons of the earth. Man did not weave the web of life; he is merely a strand in it. Whatever he does to the web, he does to himself. "*

– Ted Perry

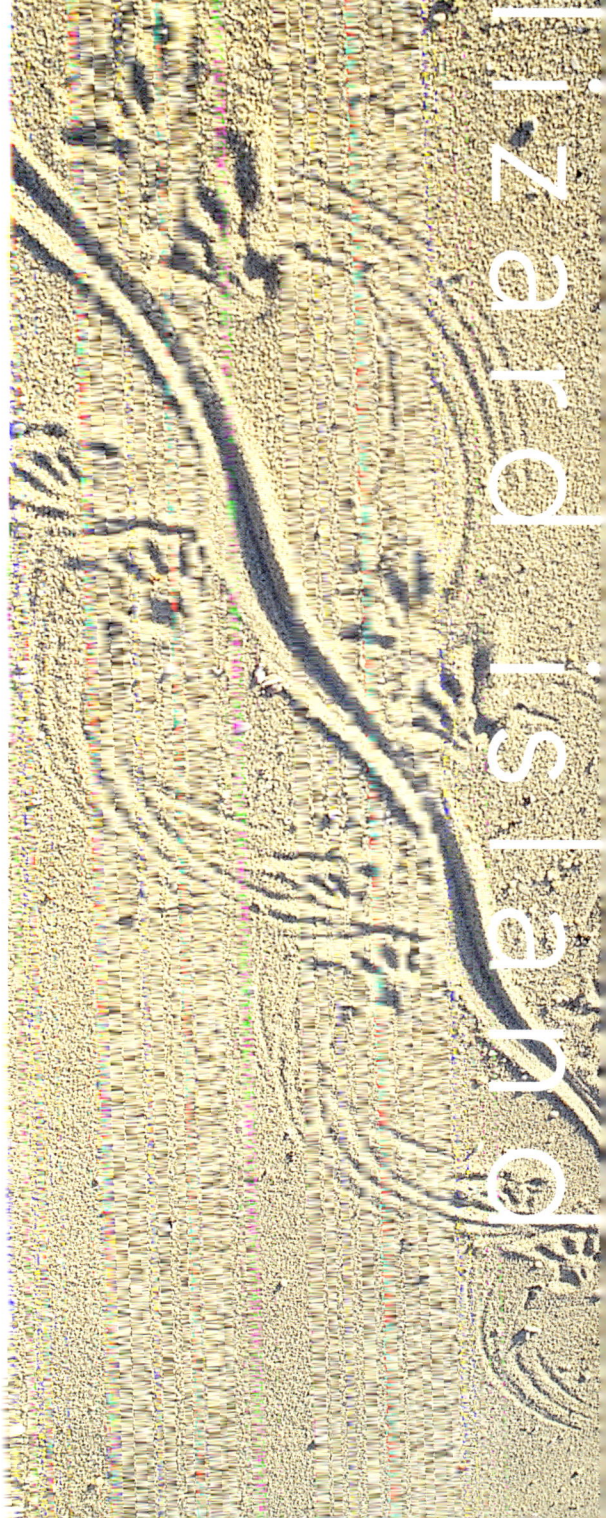

Previous page: *Wild yellow orchids set off the view from Cook's Look*
Left: *Lizard Island and its perfect Blue Lagoon*
Right: *Making tracks the Lizard way*

# solitaire

"*The only Land-animals we saw were lizards and these seem to be pretty plenty which occasioned my naming the Island ...*"

– Captain James Cook.

Moonlight cast its glow across inky-smooth waters as the *Endeavour* journeyed along the Daintree coast. The date was 11 June in the year 1770, and the ship was nearing the end of her historic voyage up the Australian coast.

As he plotted his way carefully northward through a claustrophobic labyrinth of reefs, Captain James Cook was taken by surprise as unforeseen disaster suddenly struck.

The *Endeavour* ran aground on a lonely coral outcrop some 40km north-east of a headland that Cook was later to name Cape Tribulation. There she remained for almost a day before high tides and the jettisoning of almost 50 tonnes of cargo, ballast and guns finally set her free. Fortunately, a large piece of coral broke away when the ship was refloated, plugging the breach in the *Endeavour's* hull and preventing her from sinking.

Cook's crew acted swiftly to bandage the gash with one of the ship's canvas sails, enabling the *Endeavour* to limp to shore so her crew could carry out repairs near present-day Cooktown.

Cook's despair over the troubles that plagued him is evident in his naming of prominent land features of the area. Very much alone in this untamed new world, he and his crew felt a keen sense of isolation, knowing that should they fail to salvage the vessel, they would all surely be lost.

Finally the *Endeavour* was deemed seaworthy and she sailed northward in search of open passage. Cook had expected the way ahead to be clear, but far from finding open sea, he was dismayed to see the reef encroaching ever closer towards the mainland.

In desperation *Endeavour* ventured into the waters around Lizard Island. Cook hoped that the vantage of Lizard's summit might reveal to him an escape from the clutches of the Great Barrier Reef, and so it was that "Cook's Passage" was sighted and the *Endeavour* continued homeward, carrying with her charts depicting newly discovered lands and findings that would attract European settlement and further exploration of the South Seas.

*Above: Mrs. Mary Beatrice Watson*
*Right: Preparing beche-de-mer for export to China*
*(Torres Straight Islands, 1893)*

## getting there:

Located 240km north of Cairns in Queensland and 27 km off the coast of Cape York, Lizard Island can be reached by taking a one-hour flight from Cairns. Lizard Island is a National Park covering 1,013 hectares.

Legend has it that Lizard Island was created in the Dreamtime, with the island's granite outcrops representing the body of a stingray and the smaller southern islands making up its tail.

The Dirgaal people had been visiting "Jiigurru" (Lizard Island), which was once connected to the Australian mainland by grassy plains, for some 3000 years before Cook made his "discovery". Various sites on the island reveal examples of rock art, cairns, low walls and open-ended triangles, which possibly had totemic or ceremonial significance.

The first Europeans to establish a permanent settlement on Lizard were a Scottish sea captain, Robert Watson, and his young wife Mary. They had come to Lizard with two Chinese workers to harvest beche-de-mer (sea cucumber) for export to Asian markets.

It must have seemed curious to the Dingaal people to watch them taking more than they could possibly consume from the sea, and little did the Watsons realise the anxiety their presence was causing to the Dingaal people, whose tradition dictated that trespassing or hunting without permission was an offence punishable by spearing or death.

In October 1881, when Robert was away on a fishing trip, the Aborigines landed their canoes on Lizard and attacked the two Chinese workers. One of the men was killed and the other, Ah Sam, suffered serious spear wounds. Fearing for their lives Mary, her baby Ferrier and Ah Sam fled the island in a ship's water tank, which had been used for processing the beche-de-mer. They drifted some 40 miles in eight days before finally coming to land on No. 5 Island in the Howick Group.

A passing fishing vessel reported the cottage in ruins and fires burning fiercely on Lizard, and it was assumed that Mary had been kidnapped or killed. Retaliation by police and native troopers was swift. They shot approximately 150 Cape York Aborigines, none of whom had apparently been directly involved in the incident. It was not until January the following year that the remains of Mary, her baby and Ah Sam were found and the story of their final days became clear.

Mary Watson was 21 years old when she died of thirst and exposure. Her body was discovered in the smoke-blackened tank, with the skull of baby Ferrier still resting at his mother's breast. Ah Sam had lain himself on a woven mat on the beach in the shade of a small mangrove tree. His head lay on a wooden pillow and a quilt was neatly pulled over his chest. Alongside their remains a wooden chest was found that contained Mary's diary, in which she had meticulously recorded her heart-wrenching account of their final days.

Their bodies were returned to Cooktown for burial, and a funeral procession of 650 people turned out to honour Mary's courage and spirit. In death, she came to symbolise the Australian pioneering spirit and was hailed as the epitome of a perfect settler's wife. Today the tragedy serves as a poignant example of how conflict is so often the result of misunderstanding between different cultures.

# isolation

*SERVES 2*

## INGREDIENTS

| | |
|---|---|
| 60ml | Absolut |
| 60ml | Cointreau |
| 60ml | apple & guava juice |
| | dash of lime |

## METHOD

1 Shake ingredients together.
2 Strain into lime-rimmed glass.
3 Enjoy!

# underwater snowstorm

The landscape is dominated by tussock grasslands, stunted shrubbery and sunbaked rocks sprinkled with wild yellow orchids. On first appearance it seems an austere and uninhabitable place, battered by unrelenting exposure to the elements. But on closer inspection a range of vegetation can be seen, including pockets of closed rainforest fed by perennial springs. The water source mixes with an intertidal zone where pandanus, paperbarks and mangroves flourish.

Early European settlers in Australia's tropical north set about clearing mangroves with a vengeance, seeing them as nothing more than oversized weeds in swamps teeming with disease. Little did they know that the inshore reefs are vitally dependent on mangroves as their roots filter river sediment from the water and provide refuge for juvenile reef fish.

The reef systems around Lizard Island are considered to be among Australia's best protected and diverse, due to the absence of damaging, nutrient-rich wash from coastal rivers on the mainland. Their sapphire depths support approximately 350 species of hard coral and 150 species of soft coral, as well as a bewildering array of marine creatures.

Each year, one of the most anticipated biological events on the reef takes place when the corals spawn en masse. In the northern reaches, the phenomenon occurs three or four days after the November full moon, but may be delayed until early December if the full moon occurs very early in November.

A few hours after sunset, a snowstorm of brightly coloured bundles permeates the waters. Both eggs and sperm are released by coral colonies, which spawn within seconds of each other. The spawning of an entire reef may occur over a matter of hours, and continue over three or four nights. Other invertebrates such as the Spiny Green Sea Cucumber take advantage of the moment, spawning with the corals to reduce the risk of predation.

The mix then drifts toward the surface where it forms slicks that may be hundreds of square kilometres in size. Eggs that are fertilised develop into free-swimming larvae, or planula, that drift for several days before finally settling on a reef. They cement themselves in place by building a protective limestone shell around the anemone-like polyp and by cloning the polyp become the cornerstone of a new coral colony.

*Left: A Manta Ray glides overhead as it feeds on plankton*
*Below: Silhouette of Staghorn Coral*

The fastest growing of these corals has tufts of algae, which are powered by the sun, living on the polyps. These algae tufts photosynthesise, feeding on polyp waste, and in their turn produce oxygen and up to 98 per cent of the polyp's required nutrient intake.

Like coral, the Giant Clam enjoys a symbiotic relationship with algae, which flourishes on its exposed tissue. Giant Clams grow to well in excess of one metre wide and live perhaps for centuries, but in areas of the Pacific they have become all but extinct due to over-harvesting for human consumption. Possibly the oldest and largest accessible garden of these oversized molluscs is that which may be seen in the shallow waters off Watson's Bay.

Although the Great Barrier Reef Marine Park is zoned to allow a variety of restricted commercial and recreational uses, concern remains over damage caused by commercial bottom-trawlers, which drag a heavy chain across the seabed in what is considered to be among the most destructive of fishing techniques.

Turtles and sea snakes are often an unintentional part of the trawlers' catch, and a single pass can crush between five and 25 per cent of bottom-dwelling organisms. Marine life inadvertently killed as a result of this brutal fishing method is estimated in proportions as high as 10 kilograms for every one kilogram of prawns caught.

The Great Barrier Reef is undoubtedly an invaluable asset for Australia, but its long-term wellbeing depends greatly on our ability and willingness to develop more sustainable fishing practices, and to implement policies for use of the Reef that help preserve its ecological integrity.

*Left: Colourful underwater seascape of Acropora corals*
*Right: Eyeballed by a Maori Wrasse*

## BROKENWOOD SEMILLON

From the Hunter Valley in New South Wales, Brokenwood Semillon has attractive grapefruit characters with a touch of grassiness. The subtle flavours are an excellent match for scallops.

*recommended wine*

# salad of queensland scallops

### with crispy fried fish and chili lime dressing

## INGREDIENTS

| | |
|---|---|
| 100g | reef fish |
| 100ml | peanut oil |
| 18 | fresh scallops (roe off) |
| 50ml | melted butter |

**salad**

| | |
|---|---|
| 8 | snow peas |
| 1 | Lebanese cucumber |
| ¼ bunch | frisee lettuce |
| 10 sprigs | coriander |

**dressing**

| | |
|---|---|
| 1 | large chili |
| 1 | clove garlic |
| 1 | kaffir lime leaf |
| 5 sprigs | fresh coriander |
| 100ml | fish sauce |
| 60ml | fresh lime juice |
| 5ml | sesame oil |
| 5g | caster sugar |
| 70ml | extra virgin olive oil |

## METHOD

**fish**

1  Rub fish with salt and roast until golden brown.
2  Cool, then blend in food processor until the consistency of breadcrumbs.
3  Heat peanut oil in wok until almost smoking, then add the fish and fry until the oil stops bubbling.
4  Remove and place on paper towel to drain.

**scallops**

1  Brush scallops with butter and sear in a very hot pan until white (approximately one minute).

**salad**

1  Finely slice snow peas then cut cucumber into batons lengthwise, discarding seeds.
2  Wash lettuce and coriander and pat dry with kitchen paper.
3  Toss together and set aside.

**dressing**

1  Finely chop chili, garlic, kaffir lime leaf and coriander.
2  Mix through remaining dressing ingredients.

## TO SERVE

Toss all ingredients into a bowl and serve immediately.

# endless blue

If you're hungry for adventure, then Lizard's formidable reputation as one of the world's most sought after and exclusive dive locations is something that begs investigation. Its fringing reefs are nothing short of spectacular, but for an underwater experience that will have others turning green with envy, a journey to the reef's outer edge is a must.

At the northern end of Ribbon Reef No. 10, Cod Hole is the main attraction. This is the spot for legendary encounters with giant Potato Cod, and from the moment the boat anchors the huge fish – some weighing upwards of 90kg – can be seen moving near the back of the boat.

Descending to the white, current-rippled bottom at about 10 metres it's not uncommon to sight White-tip Reef Sharks, schools of slick Barracuda, Moori Wrasse and even a Manta Ray gliding in for a peek at the activity.

A second dive site that is truly spectacular lies at the northern end of No Name Reef/Dynamite Pass. The reef wall on either side drops sharply to about 15-25 metres and is crowded with a mass of feather stars, sea squirts, sea fans and a dazzling variety of fish. To the east is the continental shelf, where ocean depths plummet to between 2000-3000 metres. Just back off the reef wall currents are fierce, and visibility in the open ocean is unlike anything imaginable. It is here that pelagic billfish like the sailfish and marlin can be

glimpsed as they flash past at speeds clocked in excess of 110km/hour.

As dusk arrives, the inhabitants of the daytime marine world reveal their true colours, creating a photographer's dream. Sharks, moray eels and octopi switch into feeding mode and Spanish Dancers stun with a gaudy display.

Impossible as it sounds, when you're finally all dived out, there are several guided interpretive nature walks that offer a great way to catch up on some land-based natural history. The Watson Bay Discovery Walk takes you from the resort, over Chinaman's Ridge and into the next valley where you have two options to explore. Turning right will lead through pandanus swamp and the local flying fox colony, whereas left takes you over the mangrove boardwalk and to the historic ruins of Mrs. Watson's cottage.

From here you can retrace Cook's steps to Lizard's summit, where "Cook's Look" offers a spectacular view over the surrounding islands and the picture-perfect Blue Lagoon. With the space to get away and explore by yourself, it's possible to forget there are other guests on the island.

The island's 24 blindingly white, powdery beaches beg exploration, and privacy is guaranteed. Island etiquette dictates that if a dinghy has already landed, the next visitors to a beach should keep motoring until another deserted stretch of sand is found.

## BANNOCKBURN SAIGNEE

**Bannockburn Saignee is a bone-dry rose made from Pinot Noir and Shiraz in Geelong, Victoria. The crisp, spicy, cherry flavours provide an interesting counterpoint to the barramundi, capsicum, olives and capers.**

recommended wine

# pan-seared baby barramundi

## with ratatouille and black olive tapenade

### INGREDIENTS

| | |
|---|---|
| 4 fillets | baby barramundi (150g each) |
| 20ml | olive oil |
| | Mizuna lettuce to garnish |
| | sea salt |

**ratatouille**

| | |
|---|---|
| 1/2 | brown onion (medium-sized, diced) |
| 1 clove | garlic |
| 1 | zucchini |
| 2 | Lebanese cucumbers |
| 2 | tomatoes |
| 1 | yellow capsicum |
| 1 | red capsicum |
| 4 | basil leaves (shredded) |
| 40ml | olive oil |

**tapenade**

| | |
|---|---|
| 50g | pitted black olives |
| 20ml | olive oil |
| 20g | capers |
| 1 | anchovy fillet |
| 1/4 bunch | parsley |
| 1 clove | garlic |
| | juice of half a lemon |
| | cracked black pepper |
| | sea salt to taste |

### METHOD

**ratatouille**

1  Finely dice onion and garlic.
2  In a saucepan, slowly fry onions and garlic in olive oil until soft.
3  Finely dice remaining vegetables then add to the pan. Cook until soft.
4  Fold through basil and season with salt and cracked pepper to taste.

**tapenade**

1  In a food processor, combine all tapenade ingredients and blend until a coarse consistency is achieved. Place to one side.

**barramundi**

1  In a frying pan, heat olive oil to a moderate to high temperature.
2  Sprinkle barramundi with sea salt and place in pan skin-side down.
3  Cook for three minutes on either side.

### TO SERVE

Place a bed of ratatouille on plate. Top with barramundi and finish with tapenade. Garnish with Mizuna lettuce.

## TALTARNI MERLOT

**Lamb and Merlot is a classic food and wine pairing. Taltarni Merlot from the Pyrenees region of Victoria is rich with mulberry/plum flavours and a velvety finish.**

# mandalong lamb

**with cauliflower puree and sweet potato gratin**

## INGREDIENTS

| | |
|---|---|
| 2 | trimmed lamb loins (200g each) |
| 10 sprigs | fresh thyme |
| 80ml | pure cream |
| 2 | sweet potatoes (medium-sized) |
| 1 | potato (medium-sized) |
| 150g | cauliflower |
| I clove | garlic (chopped) |
| 100ml | milk |
| 4 | field mushrooms |
| 1/4 bunch | watercress |
| | salt and pepper to taste |

## METHOD

### gratin

1 Finely chop four sprigs thyme, mix with cream and season with salt and pepper to taste.

2 Peel and thinly slice sweet potato and potato.

3 Arrange potatoes in a small, heavy baking dish, pour cream mixture over and sprinkle with fresh thyme.

4 Bake in oven (180°C) for 40 minutes or until cream has thickened.

### cauliflower puree

1 Wash cauliflower and remove stalks. Cut into small florets.

2 Place in saucepan with milk and chopped garlic. Simmer until soft.

3 Remove cauliflower from milk when cooked and blend in food processor until smooth.

4 Season with salt and pepper to taste.

### lamb

1 Season lamb with salt, pepper and remaining fresh thyme.

2 In a very hot pan, seal meat for approximately two minutes each side.

3 Allow to rest for five minutes before slicing (optional).

## TO SERVE

Grill mushrooms and then place on bed of cauliflower puree. Slice gratin into four even portions and position on plate alongside lamb slices. Finish with a sprig of watercress.

# stylish simplicity

*"Travel enhances the imagination. It is the longing for the exotic that stimulates the soul."*

– W. Ted Wright, AM

The Great Barrier Reef to the north of Cairns has a different character from that to the south. Flying north, it appears as an almost unbroken rampart of ribbon reefs and islands, covering some 351,400 square kilometres, or an area the size of Italy.

Lizard Island is set like a centrepiece amid languid seas. There's a strange mystique about the island, with its tragic history of adventure and romance. It seems a questionable place for settlement, but in the silence there's a powerful sense of isolation that transforms the harsh terrain into something of intriguing and hypnotic beauty.

Caressing the gentle curve of Anchor Bay, Australia's northernmost resort has been built to merge harmoniously with the environment. The architecture is a model of understatement, the buildings deliberately

unadorned so as to complement each other rather than compete with their surroundings. Floorboards are made of various polished Australian hardwoods, while the exterior timbers are of spotted gum, rough-hewn plywoods and softwoods. Villas have been built so that they are not visible above the tree line, and they have a generosity of space that matches that of their surroundings.

Anchor Bay suites are located just a stone's throw from the beach, with cool, spacious rooms that take full advantage of the view. A palette of nature's colours has been used to reflect the very essence of Australian beachside living. In each suite generous shutters open on to a large veranda where a day bed promises bliss. From the moment you arrive in your rooms there is a feeling of total relaxation, and it would be easy to idle away a week without ever feeling inclined to leave.

The resort originally opened in the 1970s as a lodge for anglers chasing big game. The new Lizard Island resort opened in July 2000, after a six-month refurbishment program. Some of the original features were retained in the lounge area, such as the distinctive rough-hewn granite walls, the flip of a marlin's tail and a colonnaded veranda that opens to satiny seas.

The relaxed, yet stylish Osprey's Restaurant is the hub for the resort's discerning clientele. The hot, tropical climate dictates a menu that changes daily and features a simplicity that is shaped by a diversity of cultural cuisines. Using only the finest in fresh seafood and tropical fruits, each dish is enhanced by the chef's unique creative style and contemporary flair.

A dreamy way to rejuvenate is to be transported at the Pavilion Spa. Treatments reflect the island's natural beauty, harnessing all that is known from the past and all that is known in the present to bring about a total harmony of health, beauty and nature. On offer is a range of sacred Indian, beautifying Oriental and ancient Aboriginal treatments that embody the essence of Lizard and harness the purity of the environment.

Sea Elements is one of the island's popular treatments. It begins with a full body exfoliation that prepares the

skin for an application of marine extract gel. An extra-
fine marine algae poultice body-wrap then follows,
facilitating absorption of nutrients from the product.
The treatment is relaxing while detoxifying, allowing
intensive remineralisation of the skin.

Lizard's environmentally sensitive management policy
nurtures the original character of the island, and in the
evenings you may hear the little "tick, tick, tick" of
geckos that help keep insect numbers down. They
compete for attention with the island's most
conspicuous reptile, the Yellow Spotted Sand Monitor
Lizard, otherwise known as the Goanna.

Although numerous these creatures are harmless by
nature and amble about the island excavating cool
hollows with their strong-clawed legs. Growing to over
one and a half metres in length, they make a comical
sight awkwardly hauling their bulk into villa footbaths,
which they seem to think have been placed around the
resort as private swimming pools for goannas.

The Lizard Island Research Station was established in
1973 by the Australian Museum to further existing
knowledge of the Great Barrier Reef. The station
carries out approximately 60 research projects
annually, and joining one of the resort's station tours
offers guests the chance to learn about the latest
research being conducted around the island. Funded

by fees from visiting
scientists, and
donations from
individuals and
organisations, it has
grown from a series of
tents near the beach to
its present-day form.

## PELORUS NV

**An alternative to dessert wine with a dish such as this is an intense sparkling wine, and Pelorus Non Vintage from Cloudy Bay in New Zealand is perfect with its creamy, citric characters.**

# marbled chocolate and grand marnier cheesecake

## INGREDIENTS

| | |
|---|---|
| 4 | pre-made tuille/brandy snap baskets |

### cheesecake

| | |
|---|---|
| 170g | cream cheese |
| 60g | caster sugar |
| | egg yolk |
| 2 tsp | gelatin powder |
| 20ml | warm water |
| 140ml | cream (lightly whipped) |
| 45g | dark chocolate |
| 110g | white chocolate |
| 40ml | Grand Marnier |
| | shaved dark chocolate for garnish |
| 4 scoops | icecream |

## METHOD

1. In a food processor, whip cream cheese and caster sugar until smooth.
2. Add egg yolk and continue to mix for a further three minutes.
3. Melt gelatin in warm water.
4. Lightly whip cream and fold through the gelatin.
5. Add the cream cheese and gelatin mixtures together and divide them equally into two bowls.
6. Melt the two chocolates separately and fold the Grand Marnier through the white chocolate.
7. Carefully fold white chocolate through one part of cream cheese mix and dark chocolate through the other part.
8. Slowly fold the dark and the white chocolate mixes together to achieve a marbled effect.
9. Staple clear plastic strips (15cm long x 6cm wide) together to form round moulds and sit on to plates.
10. Fill moulds with mixture and place in fridge for two hours to set.

## TO SERVE

Remove moulds, garnish with shaved chocolate. Place one scoop of your favourite icecream into each tuille basket and top with berry or fruit sauce.

*I am the eternal traveller, Badu – the dreamer, the fool. A travelling soul. Let me walk the plains of this earth, the valleys, the desolated deserts, the endless seas. I'll rest later.*

– Yossi Ghinsberg

# index of recipes

# metric conversions

## Weight Measurements

| standard US | ounces | metric |
|---|---|---|
| 1 ounce | 1 | 30 grams |
| 1/4 pound | 4 | 125 grams |
| 1/2 pound | 8 | 250 grams |
| 1 pound | 16 | 500 grams |
| 1 1/2 pounds | 24 | 750 grams |
| 2 pounds | 32 | 1 kilogram |
| 2 1/2 pounds | 40 | 1.25 kilograms |
| 3 pounds | 48 | 1.5 kilograms |

## Volume Measurements

| standard US | ounces | metric |
|---|---|---|
| 1 tablespoon | 1/2 | 15 millilitres |
| 2 tablespoons | 1 | 30 millilitres |
| 3 tablespoons | 1 1/2 | 45 millilitres |
| 1/4 cup | 2 | 60 millilitres |
| 6 tablespoons | 3 | 90 millilitres |
| 1/2 cup | 4 | 125 millilitres |
| 1 cup | 8 | 250 millilitres |
| 1 pint (2 cups) | 16 | 500 millilitres |
| 4 cups (1 quart) | 32 | 1 litre |

## Oven Temperature

| fahrenheit | celsius |
|---|---|
| 300° | 150° |
| 325° | 165° |
| 350° | 180° |
| 375° | 190° |
| 400° | 200° |
| 425° | 220° |
| 450° | 230° |

## Alternative Seafood

The following may be substituted if Australian varieties are unavailable.

Coral Trout – Sea Bass or other white-fleshed reef fish

Ocean Trout – Atlantic Salmon or other pink-fleshed fish.

Barramundi – Nile Perch.

Moreton Bay Bugs – Prawns or Shrimp.

# acknowledgements

When the thought to produce this book first struck, I was enjoying one of the most fabulous holidays ever. I was on Heron Island, the turtles were running, the manta rays friendly in their curiosity and my partner had become carried away by the sunset and proposed.

The months that followed were a whirlwind of planning – none of it for a wedding. P&O Australian Resorts had the courage to buy into my dream and sent me packing around their portfolio of beautiful resorts on a journey of discovery.

Darren Jew and his 45kg of camera gear accompanied me to many of the resorts and, despite his habit of dragging me up too many mountains well before sunrise and using me as bait for mosquitos, it is largely thanks to his untiring efforts that I feel we have managed to capture the essence of each location.

The two things that struck me most during our travels were the same two things that prompted me to produce this book. They were; an absolute amazement at the amount of wildlife that flourished in the grounds of the resorts and the consistency of high-quality cuisine. Although difficult to communicate in print, I hope that in some small way we've managed to capture a little of the magic that may be found at each of the resorts and lodges.

My sincere thanks goes to the resort General Managers, Assistant General Managers and their dedicated teams. Thanks especially to the executive chefs; Peter Stalder, Paul Huxtable, Tony Kramer, Laurent Pedemay and Mark Long, as well as to Daniel Smith and Geoff Clark, who re-created the culinary wonders on behalf of their associates.

Thank you also to Valda Winsor and Hazel Douglas, who shared their precious memories with me, and to Susan Whitehead for gently guiding me in documenting each area's natural and cultural history.

To all of the photographers – especially Gary Bell, Mike McCoy, Chris Chen, Rob Blakers, Peter McConchie, Garth McLaomainn and Peter Jarver – who helped us to catch the dream by supplying their exquisite images.

Finally; special thanks to P&O's Craig Bradbery and Shelly Parer for their help with project logistics. And to Sharon Serci, for learning so quickly how to end my sentences and intuitively translate the vision that was knocking around in my head into a design that I feel is second to none.

# picture credits